THE EMOTIONS GOD GAVE YOU

A GUIDE FOR CATHOLICS TO HEALTHY AND HOLY LIVING

The Emotions God Gave You

A Guide for Catholics to Healthy and Holy Living

Art and Laraine Bennett

the WORD among us® Press

Published by The Word Among Us Press
7115 Guilford Drive
Frederick, MD 21704

15 14 13 12 11   1 2 3 4 5

ISBN: 978-1-59325-185-7

Scripture texts in this work are taken from the *New American Bible with Revised New Testament and Revised Psalms*, copyright © 1991, 1986, 1970, Confraternity of Christian Doctrine, Washington, DC and are used by permission of the copyright owner. All rights reserved. No part of the *New American Bible* may be reproduced in any form without permission in writing from the copyright owner.

Excerpts from the English translation of the *Catechism of the Catholic Church* for use in the United States of America, copyright © 1994, United States Catholic Conference, Inc.—Libreria Editrice Vaticana. Used with permission.

Note: All the examples used in this book are composites of real-life situations, in which the names and identifying details have been changed to protect confidentiality. The stories are meant to represent universal truths about our emotional lives, so the features may seem familiar.

Cover design by Faceout Studio

Made and printed in the United States of America

Library of Congress Cataloging-in-Publication Data

Bennett, Art.
  The emotions God gave you : a guide for Catholics to healthy and holy living / Art and Laraine Bennett.
    p. cm.
  Includes bibliographical references.
  ISBN 978-1-59325-185-7
  1. Emotions—Religious aspects—Catholic Church. 2. Christian life—Catholic authors. I. Bennett, Laraine. II. Title.
  BX2350.3.B463 2011
  233'.5--dc22
                                              2011005370

For Lianna, Ray and Laura, Sam, and Lucy

Acknowledgments

We are deeply grateful to Father Emmerich Vogt, OP, for his friendship and his wisdom. His talks and writings helped us understand the critical role of emotions in healthy Christian living. We also thank Patty Mitchell, our editor, whose insight and thorough editing helped make this book a reality.

The good herein is through the grace of God; the mistakes are our own.

Contents

Foreword

It is not uncommon for people to confess their feelings and emotions as if they were sinful in and of themselves. The *Catechism of the Catholic Church* explains that the passions—feelings and emotions—have no moral value in themselves (CCC, 1767). They are not morally good, nor are they morally bad. What gives them a moral component is what we do about them. All sin lies in the will—in what a person freely chooses to do. By exercising free will, a person can sanctify his feelings in acting virtuously or pervert them with vice. This is a crucial truth for a Christian to embrace in order to know and understand himself. And this is what makes Art and Laraine Bennett's latest book so important.

Since the will is dependent on the intellect to make its decisions, it is important to know the truth. As St. Thomas Aquinas explains, sin darkens the intellect. We are born with a wound that keeps us in darkness unless we are enlightened. So we say that Christ is the light that came into the darkness to help us see the truth (John 8:12). Jesus tells us of the man born blind (John 9:1-41) as a way of referring to the fallen state of all the wounded children of Eve. "Know the truth," says Christ, "and the truth will set you free" (John 8:32). By knowing the truth about ourselves and our emotions, we can discover ways to mature and, as Art and Laraine write, "gain the emotional equilibrium and healthy balance we need to take charge of our lives, grow closer to Christ, and share in the joy of his love."

The relevance of *The Emotions God Gave You* is evident. Without a proper understanding of the important role played by our passions, we are truly left in the dark. When people are afraid of owning their emotions, they wear a mask. And if a person denies his feelings, he acts them out. When a person neglects to understand how emotional responses are affected by his background and temperament, he is often left feeling hopeless and even despairing because of unwanted feelings. The Bennetts do a great service to the Christian community—indeed, to any person of good will—by explicating the role of emotions and pointing the way to emotional equilibrium.

Emotions are part of our human existence whereby "man intuits the good and suspects evil" (CCC, 1771). But our emotions need to mature because, as the Bennetts show, a person's temperament, his inner wounds, and his life experiences profoundly influence his emotional responses. A person in his spiritual journey needs to learn how to mature his emotions and achieve an emotional equilibrium such that his emotions do not make his decisions for him. Rather, he is in control of his responses no matter what emotions come into play.

With common examples from everyday living, the Bennetts offer us a deepened understanding of this most important aspect of human living. Ignoring or denying how we feel has serious consequences. The Bennetts show how adequate self-understanding enables us to recognize when we are acting out of an emotional bias. We only have to look at the daily news to see how so many adults are controlled by their emotions and respond in inappropriate ways to threatening situations because they have never learned to mature their emotions.

As a person who grew up in a family with addiction and mental illness—and therefore has learned of the need for effective healing of the emotions—I have great admiration for this work by Art and Laraine Bennett. This book could not have come at a better time given our current lack of a lucid study on the emotions in light of Christian theology. All who avail themselves of this straightforward presentation of the role of emotions in the moral life of the Christian will greatly benefit from the wealth of understanding it presents. It enlightens the way to Christian health and holiness. The Bennetts' book brings clear insights into human behavior vis-à-vis the emotions. It is a relief to learn, for example, and as the Church teaches (CCC, 1768), that "strong feelings are not decisive for the morality or the holiness of persons." Good, holy people have a wide expanse of emotions. For example, a saintly and morally chaste person can have deep sexual feelings. The feelings themselves say nothing about the holiness of the person. As the Bennetts so cogently demonstrate, we are not to suppress our emotions but to guide them by reason and will. Because emotions are a fundamental part of human life, they need to be directed by grace.

It is surprising that many modern manuals of spiritual direction tend to neglect the role of emotions in human life. This neglect can defeat a person's desire for wholeness. St. Thomas Aquinas knew this well when he taught, "Being insensitive to our feelings and emotions is a vice" (IIa IIæ, Q. 92 A1). As a result, his study on the moral life includes a section on the emotions. The emotional life, which forms a part of our being, has a place in moral reflection, for man does not work out his destiny solely by acts of his free will. Rather, it is with the power of his whole being, body and soul, that he attains his salvation. The Bennetts' serious reflection on the role of the emotions makes this evident. Those who immerse themselves in *The Emotions God Gave You* will find a necessary guide to healthy and holy living.

Fr. Emmerich Vogt, OP
Founder, *The Twelve-Step Review*

INTRODUCTION

We have all had the experience of being overcome with emotion. We may have wept over a loved one's death, been swept away by an uplifting tide of joy, felt shock at an unusual or startling event, or experienced rage that seemed nearly uncontrollable. We may have been suddenly enveloped by bone-chilling dread or fear. And, of course, we have all experienced love—especially love for a spouse, parent, or child.

Less intense emotions also accompany our daily thoughts and activities. Perhaps we were pleasantly surprised upon finding a letter from a friend in the mailbox. We may have been disappointed by a missed opportunity. A feeling of calmness may have settled over us as we entered a church. In fact, it is likely that every action, thought, and decision we have is accompanied by some emotion—whether or not we are consciously aware of it![1]

The Church has traditionally called emotions like anger, fear, or love the "passions," from the Latin word *passio* ("to undergo," "to suffer"), because we undergo a change as we experience them. It almost seems as though we are the passive recipients of emotions, that we can't help ourselves when we are overcome by fear, anger, anxiety, happiness, sadness, or love. We say, "I fell in love" or "He was engulfed by rage" or "I was overcome with sadness," as though we had no control over our feelings.

It is quite true that most often our emotions arise in us spontaneously—at times, even unconsciously. We may snipe at someone without even fully realizing that we are angry, or we may feel

inexplicably drawn to someone without realizing why. The imme-
diacy and spontaneity of our emotions are among the ways in
which emotions ensure our survival. For example, the fear that
triggers our jumping out of the way of a speeding car—before we
even have time to think through the best course of action—can
save our life. Sexual desire is likely built into us so that we will
reproduce. An intense feeling of revulsion when we smell a foul
odor is a built-in warning signal. There are also psychic emotional
responses that are beneficial: anger when we see an injustice, for
example, or tender love for a new baby.

Yet even though our emotions seem to arise in us unbidden,
without our directly willing them (and sometimes even against
our will), we are nonetheless capable of managing or regulating them. For example, a soldier appropriately experiences fear
because he is in danger. But because he is well trained, he main-
tains his post, despite his feelings. Or although a mother might
feel her anger rising when her child interrupts her, she refrains
from unleashing her anger in harsh words. Though feelings of
anger or sadness or desire arise in us spontaneously, we are
free to respond in any number of ways. The Catholic Church
teaches that passions (or emotions) are neither good nor evil in
themselves, but they can become so when the *will* is engaged;
that is, the way I *choose* to behave can be considered to be
moral or immoral. If the soldier left his post out of fear or the
mother lashed out with angry and hurtful words, they may be
morally culpable. If the mother stops to think before yelling at
the child who interrupts her, then she is acting rationally. Our
reason should govern our passions. (*Catechism of the Catholic
Church* [CCC], 1767).

However, reason alone is not always sufficient to change our emotional patterns, especially if they are deeply engrained or the product of past emotional wounds. We may need help from counselors and confessors. When we feel stymied or paralyzed by unwanted or debilitating emotions that may have arisen due to a past trauma, or perhaps simply because of a pattern or habit we have fallen into, we are *less free* to act in a healthy way, and we are less capable of having fulfilling relationships. We may feel oppressed by our own moods, fears, and anxieties, or we may push people away through our anger and resentment. These are obstacles to happy, healthy, and holy living. We hope this book will offer some insight into the ways that our emotions can help (or hinder) healthy living as well as some new ways of managing them.

The Emotions God Gave You is not meant to outline a definitive theory of emotion or to choose sides in a competition of therapies or strategies to deal with our sometimes unruly emotions. Rather, with each chapter we hope to help paint a picture of the richness of the emotional life, each chapter adding a layer of color to the portrait. In the following pages, we will look at how emotions affect us and how our thoughts, attitudes, and behavior can affect our emotions. We'll also examine the difference between emotion and mood, and explore the consequences of anger and resentment. What are the effects of temperament and our past experiences on our emotional health? Can we trust our feelings? When do our emotions become destructive? How do past emotional wounds affect our present-day emotional balance? What does it mean, practically speaking, for our reason to govern our passions? Finally, we will discuss ways to have a healthy emotional life, gain self-mastery, and grow in virtue and holiness. After all, God gave us our emotions. He wants us to manage them for our own good—and for his glory!

Art and Laraine Bennett

CHAPTER 1

WHAT ARE EMOTIONS?

It is just as wrong to despise all emotions as to advocate
their unrestrained activity.

—Joseph Massman

Why do humans have emotions? Human beings have feelings and emotions because we are physical beings. From medieval times, theologians and now neuroscientists have understood emotions to involve a physiological process (the precise nature of which is hotly debated).[2] For example, anger involves an elevated heart rate. Fear may involve trembling or shortness of breath. Theologians have argued that purely spiritual beings (for example, angels) do not have feelings or emotions. St. Thomas Aquinas further argued that God, being perfect and therefore incapable of suffering, does not have emotions per se. God loves and shows mercy but only insofar as they are acts of the divine will, not as feelings or bodily sensations or in any way indicating a lack in God's perfection. Furthermore, says St. Thomas, while Scripture refers to God as being angry or wrathful, these emotions are attributed to him metaphorically.[3] Of course, Jesus Christ, in his human nature, did have emotions.

We are not angels or pure spirits, but neither are we purely material beings, as some scientists would like to insist. We are, as St. Paul wrote, body, mind, and spirit (1 Thessalonians 5:23).[4] On the most basic level, feelings are basic instincts like pain, hunger, or the need to sleep. These physical feelings are important for survival, and we need to pay attention to them. But we also experience "psychic feelings" or emotions, such as fear or hatred when I perceive evil, and love and joy when I perceive the good. Feelings or passions are forces that *motivate* us to pursue the good or avoid evil (CCC, 1763). Our feelings are natural, an important part of being human, and vital in our pursuit of the good. When our emotions are directed toward the good—toward God—they become spiritually beneficial. We experience *delight* in God's word, *sorrow* for sin, *compassion* for our fellow man, *hunger* for justice, and *joy* in his presence—all vitally part of our loving God *with all our heart*, as we are commanded by Christ (Mark 12:30; Luke 10:27).

THE IMPORTANCE OF EMOTIONS

Emotions are critical, not only for our survival, but also for thriving as human beings. Fear warns us about a threat to our personal safety; love accompanies our intimate relationships. In fact, emotions provide us with important information about our relationships and our environment. As signals to ourselves and others, they help us to monitor our relationships and allow us to reveal our deepest needs to our loved ones. They also motivate us for action.

Our actions, thoughts, and decisions are almost always influenced or accompanied by emotions, even when we are not fully aware of them. They are the "motive forces" of the soul.[5] However, emotions can arise in us due to a conscious decision as well. For example, if I see someone acting rudely toward an elderly person, I might consciously give in to a righteous anger and speak out. Thus, emotions can arise in us both unconsciously and consciously.

It is not healthy to completely suppress our emotions, nor is it always possible to "control" them (more on this in a later chapter). However, we can (and should) be *aware* of them, and identify the most prudent way of dealing with them. We are free to choose how we *respond* to our feelings. In fact, we human beings function best when we act and think *reasonably*. Do we allow our passions to rule us, or does reason guide us? Do we feed our anger or resentment? Are we steeped in bitterness or envy? Do we wallow in self-pity? Are we incapacitated by fear? Do we judge others based on past resentments or emotional wounds? In short, it is wise to regulate, or manage, our emotions in light of reason.

It takes self-knowledge to recognize when we are acting out of an emotional bias. Having a well-balanced personality and being emotionally mature requires becoming aware of our emotions, knowing whether they are appropriate or inappropriate to the situation, and then responding rationally.

In themselves, our emotions are morally neutral (CCC, 1767). However, what we *do* with our emotions can be judged to be good or bad. The soldier who acted out of his fear and deserted his post may be considered to have acted wrongly. His fear was not wrong, but his actions were. Deliberately stirring up feelings of hatred for another person, seeking revenge, or dwelling on lustful thoughts is very likely to be sinful. "Passions are morally good when they contribute to a good action, evil in the opposite case" (CCC, 1768). We can understand this better when we consider the *object* of our emotions. If my desire is directed toward serving God and neighbor, it is good. If my desire is to view pornography, it is sinful.

Because he was true man, Jesus had feelings. He became quite angry with the Pharisees (Mark 3:5) and with the money changers outside the temple (Matthew 21:12-13). Just before Jesus performed the miracle of the loaves and fish to feed the hungry crowd, the gospel tells us that "his heart was moved with pity for them" (Mark 6:34). Jesus cried when Lazarus died (John 11:35), and as he approached Jerusalem prior to his crucifixion, "he saw the city and wept over it" (Luke 19:41). He was in agony and distress in the Garden of Gethsemane the night before he was crucified—so much so that he sweated blood (Luke 22:44) and said, "My soul is sorrowful even to death" (Matthew 26:38). Jesus experienced the utmost desolation and abandonment on the cross: "My God, my God, why have you forsaken me?" (Matthew 27:46). Christ's emotions were always perfectly appropriate for the situation. His anger toward the Pharisees was justified, and his sorrow about Lazarus's death was entirely real, an outpouring of grief and love for his dear friend.

Emotions before and after the Fall

Because of original sin, our emotions are not always appropriate to the situation. They are not always balanced or guided by reason; worse, they can sometimes usurp reason! We may let our emotions get out of hand or make decisions emotionally instead of rationally. We may have a violent temper or suffer from anxiety. We may be subject to mood swings or depression. We may be emotionally overwrought or we may be overly cool and withdrawn.

It wasn't always this way. In the Garden of Eden prior to the Fall, Adam and Eve were perfectly balanced. They were in complete harmony with God, with each other, and with all of creation. God walked with them in the garden, "at the breezy time of the day" (Genesis 3:8). They were intelligent immortal lords of the world.[6]

Adam and Eve's relationship with each other was also harmonious. They did not argue; they were not jealous or suspicious, nor did they try to dominate one another. They were perfectly suited to each other—best friends and perfect partners. When the Pharisees asked Jesus why Moses allowed divorce, he told them that it was because of the "hardness of your hearts," but that "from the beginning it was not so" (Matthew 19:8). Adam's and Eve's emotions were in perfect harmony with their minds and wills. In this state of what theologians call "original justice," our first parents had perfect control over their passions. There were no internal battles over whether to eat that last slice of cake, nor did they ever fly off the handle in a fit of temper.[7]

But the devil sowed suspicion in their hearts and tempted them with the prospect of being "like gods who know what is good and what is bad" (Genesis 3:5). Adam and Eve turned away from God as their loving Father. When they disobeyed God, they created a rift, not only between them and God, but between each other. Now they were suspicious of each other. Adam blamed Eve, and they both became ashamed. Enmity between men and women entered the world.

The result is that now, not only do we often feel distant from God and misunderstood by other people, but we also no longer possess that harmonious balance within our own psyche. Our intellect is darkened, our wills weakened. Our passions can get out of control. Even though we are baptized, we still experience the effects of original sin: "I do not do the good I want, but I do the evil I do not want" (Romans 7:19).

Our emotions can range from superficial sentimentality to a deep, abiding love for God and true sorrow for sin. Our emotions can move us in compassion toward our neighbor and in holy rejoicing in the Lord. But our emotions can also lead us to sin: lust, envy, and greed. We can also be victims of our moods. We have all had the experience of waking up on top of the world only to come crashing down as our mood changes, like a thundercloud rolling in to sweep the sun out of our life. We don't want to be as fickle as a weather vane, spinning and turning with every gust of wind. Rather, we would like our actions to be based on principles; we do the *right thing*, no matter what our mood or how we feel about it.

Managing Our Emotions

How rewarding it can be to *manage* our emotions—not suppressing or ignoring them! We can seek a healthy balance in our emotional lives, directed ultimately toward God. When we examine ourselves and our own emotional tendencies, we can then take the next step to gain equilibrium and to regulate (and perhaps even transform) our emotions and moods. In fact, "training our emotions to respond to the direction of reason is a most difficult task, and its achievement is called virtue."[8]

As long as there is no serious handicap (whether physical or psychological) that would require professional guidance, we can gradually improve ourselves and grow in emotional stability and maturity through a deep interior life. As we shed our unhealthy attachments (more on this in chapter 9), we become more free to love God and our neighbor purely and joyfully. The more we get to know Christ through prayer and the sacraments, the greater our love for him. And the greater our attachment to him, to what is truly good, the less we will find ourselves swayed by unwelcome moods, unhealthy attachments, or violent passions. Christ himself is the healer who will direct our passions, helping us to achieve harmony within our souls. Our hearts will be free to respond with lightness and peace to God's boundless grace.

When our emotions prompt us toward greater love of God and neighbor, we are growing in holiness. But when our moods are up and down like a roller coaster or our emotions are flying out of control, we can become a cross for our friends and family, and we may fail to respond to God's will. It is wise to take a personal inventory of our emotional well-being: Do I tend to overreact when someone says a slightly hurtful comment? Am I anxious, moody, or fretful? Do I easily fly off the handle and become angry? Do I continue to dwell on my angry feelings, feeding bitterness and resentment in my soul? Do I give up when my mood changes? Do I indulge myself in my passions or moods? Do I ride a roller coaster of emotions, sometimes cheerful and other times despondent? Am I constantly finding fault? Do I indulge in self-pity? Can I laugh at myself? It is wise to know ourselves—how we tend to react, our prevailing mood, and how our emotions influence us. With this knowledge, we will be better able to make prudent choices and wise decisions and to respond more freely to God's grace.

Wise spiritual directors, saints, and spiritual writers over the centuries have offered many insights into ways of managing our emotions so that they work harmoniously in our lives for the purpose of drawing us closer to God. Among these are recognizing our dependence on God, placing ourselves in his presence, praying daily, and receiving the sacraments frequently. But the saints often begin with self-knowledge. Knowing ourselves and our tendencies will allow us to better regulate our reactions and our emotions. Ultimately, this self-knowledge, along with a deep interior life, ongoing conversion, and dependence on God's mercy, will result in a calm acceptance of ourselves and others as well as genuine joy, trust in God, and true charity. Moodiness, oversensitivity, self-pity, fear, anger, and resentment, constant fault finding or blaming—all these can lead to sins against charity. When we achieve a healthy emotional balance, we will be more capable of responding generously to God's will and benevolently toward our neighbor.

"He brought me into the wine cellar, he set in order charity in me," says the bride in the Song of Songs (2:4).[9] After the Fall, our psyche became disordered, and with it, our emotions and impulses. But it is Christ, the bridegroom and the beloved, who will order our souls according to his all-consuming love. The closer we grow to Jesus, the greater our inner harmony will be and the more love and peace will reign in our hearts.

Our hope is that by better understanding our emotions and discovering ways to manage and even transform them,[10] we will gain the emotional equilibrium and healthy balance we need to take charge of our lives, grow closer to Christ, and share in the joy of his love.

GOING FURTHER

1. What emotions do you struggle with? Do unruly emotions cause strife in your family, with your spouse or children, or in your relationship with God? Do you need to feel "in the mood" to pray or to serve others joyfully?

2. St. Paul writes to the Philippians: "Rejoice in the Lord always! . . . Have no anxiety at all, but in everything, by prayer and petition, with thanksgiving, make your requests known to God. Then the peace of God that surpasses all understanding will guard your hearts and minds in Christ Jesus" (4:4, 6-7). What is Paul telling us about attaining peace and joy? When you are able to put everything in the hands of God—with thanksgiving—do you experience true peace and joy? Does something keep you from letting go of those feelings of anxiety, fear, sadness, anger, or bitterness?

3. Studies have shown that people who are grateful, forgiving, and generous are happier. (We discuss this in more detail in chapter 6.) How do you think these virtues contribute to your overall mood?

4. Sometimes when we dwell too long on our problems, we feel as though we are going down a rabbit hole with no exit, and we can become anxious or depressed. On the other hand, if we ignore our problems, they are unlikely to improve. What is your tendency? What might be a way to strike a healthy balance in your life?

5. Reflect on a time when you were truly passionate about something or someone. How much more energy and focus did you have? Were you able to overcome obstacles easily? How can you harness that same passion to grow in holiness?

CHAPTER 2

EMOTIONS AND TEMPERAMENT

We boil at different degrees.

—Ralph Waldo Emerson

We were running late for school again when Laraine realized that she had forgotten to make a lunch for our youngest daughter. "Oh, don't worry, Mom," Lucy said,. "I'll just borrow some money from my friends." This response was typical of Lucy, yet such a contrast to her older sister, who would have been paralyzed by the proposition of no lunch. The difference between our two daughters was also noted by the German teacher who taught both girls in high school. Our eldest was a studious perfectionist while her younger sister was more interested in chatting with her classmates. Their differences are an aspect of their unique temperaments.[11]

Let's take another example. Laraine is driving 60 miles per hour on the freeway when someone cuts sharply in front of her, nearly causing an accident. She honks and yells at the man, shaking her fist. Art has a similar experience, yet he makes no response—that is, until later, when he's at work and realizes that he might have been killed. Then he breaks into a cold sweat. Both Art and Laraine had reactions to a similar incident, but they expressed them differently.

Temperament is our "genetically-based emotional disposition"[12]—the way we tend to react emotionally. It is part of our nature, our biological constitution. Essentially, some people tend to react quickly (or slowly), intensely (or not intensely), or to be more (or less) sociable, particularly in new situations. Some people are naturally easygoing and calm; others are easily aroused or emotionally volatile. One person may be more passionate while another person is more laid-back. One individual is extremely sensitive while another may be rather thick-skinned. This is the way we are "hardwired." From birth we are sensitive, tranquil, or anxious. Just as some people are taller or shorter, brown-eyed or blue, so too they are more or less optimistic or pessimistic, dependent or independent, conscientious or careless, suspicious or trusting.[13]

Differences in temperament profoundly affect how each of us reacts to the individual circumstances of our lives. Depending on my temperament, I may tend to respond to stressful situations in anger or withdrawal. I may have difficulty letting go of wounded feelings or anxious thoughts. These are all aspects of our God-given temperament. Many temperament traits are evident at birth and persist throughout childhood and even into adulthood. For example, studies conducted on babies as young as four months of age identified temperamental traits such as high or low reactivity. Babies who were identified as being highly reactive, or anxious, around strangers or with new experiences often expressed a similar anxiety as young adults when confronting new situations.[14] The landmark thirty-year longitudinal study by psychiatrists Alexander Thomas and Stella Chess identified lasting temperament traits of persistence, distractibility, intensity, mood, adaptability, and activity, among others.[15]

Of course, our emotional responses are also influenced by our environment and life experiences. Someone who survived a war or who lived through a depression will be profoundly affected by those experiences. Similarly, someone who lost a parent at a young age, suffered ongoing abuse, or grew up in an alcoholic family may find his or her emotional life altered through those experiences. (We discuss this in greater depth in chapter 8.) Even our culture can have an impact on our emotional bias.[16] Some cultures seem to "favor" a certain temperamental style: Researchers found that Asian infants showed greater placidity and less reactivity to unexpected events, cried less when inoculated, and were less distressed by having their arms restrained than did Caucasian infants.[17]

But temperament profoundly impacts our emotional responses. It is important to note that given a very frightening or highly stressful situation, most everyone will be (appropriately) upset; however, depending on their temperament, some may be significantly more upset or become highly anxious, and they may not be able to calm themselves down for quite some time. Some people may have an unusually strong reaction to a *less* stressful situation or may fail to respond initially but suddenly become agitated or upset later. These are all aspects of temperament—temperamental "biases" that are physiologically based. In other words, our bodies are "biologically prepared" to be susceptible to certain feelings.[18]

Because our emotions (and even our general mood) are greatly influenced by our temperament, it is helpful to understand the role temperament plays in our emotional life.

TEMPERAMENTS IN ACTION

"Nora"[19] is a young mom with three children under the age of six. She is sensitive and thoughtful, but lately she has been feeling particularly overwhelmed. The laundry and dishes seem to pile up, the kids seem inordinately needy and combative with one another, and her husband often comes home late from the office. She finds herself screaming at the children and complaining to her husband as soon as he walks through the door. Life seems chaotic and stuck in an endless cycle of messes, yelling, and tears. To make matters worse, Nora compares herself to her highly competent sister-in-law who has five children, volunteers at church, and runs a home-based business. Her sister-in-law is rarely stressed and seems to have everything under control. Nora feels like a failure and wonders if there is something wrong with her.[20]

In fact, Nora is a sensitive and thoughtful *melancholic*. She feels deeply and intensely, and is also somewhat reticent, introverted, and rather pessimistic. She does not always express her deep interior emotions and thoughts. Her sister-in-law, with boundless energy and an unfailingly positive "can-do" attitude, is *choleric*. When Nora's sister-in-law is faced with chaos, she turns into General Patton and starts rallying the troops. When Nora faces a similar situation, she wants to cry.

Temperament plus situation "fit together like a lock and key to release an emotional reaction."[21] A melancholic who is in a stressful situation may have a stronger, more intense emotional response (tears, anxiety, fear) than a person with another temperament.

Most of our emotional tendencies (even our moods) are due to our God-given temperament. The choleric tends to have quick and intense reactions focused on the present—making him decisive, driven, and passionate about his pursuits. In a stressful situation, he is more likely to react with anger or action than with tears or anxiety. The choleric is a go-getter, your classic type A personality, a confident and often extraverted individual who loves to take charge of situations.

The *phlegmatic* temperament is the exact opposite of the choleric: peaceful, easygoing, and calm. The emotional life of a phlegmatic is steady and understated; he is never too high or too low, and his reactions are almost always even-keeled. He rarely gets angry or raises his voice. He is quiet, cooperative, well-balanced, controlled, and reliable. In fact, he can be so cooperative and so willing to create harmony that he denies his own wishes and makes compromises that (over time) can lead to resentment if he does not attend to his own feelings.

The *sanguine*, on the other hand, has quick and intense—but short-lived—reactions. He easily expresses his emotions (he is the most extraverted of all the temperaments), and he does not hold on to negative feelings. He tends to be emotionally upbeat and positive. He is the classic "people person"—talkative, outgoing, and sociable. The sanguine is affectionate, fun-loving, and enthusiastic. He struggles for self-control as his emotions and lively curiosity often get the better of him. But overall, his mood tends to be cheerful.

The melancholic is 180 degrees from the sanguine. His emotions may be slow to rise to the surface, but they are deep and long lasting—and very vehement—when they do appear. He tends to be very introverted, thoughtful, reflective, and self-sacrificing. He is persevering and pursues the noblest ideals. Because he is the most introverted, his emotional reactions are often delayed and may relate to the past or future (recalling a past negative incident or worrying about a future possibility). Thus, he may be more susceptible to fear, anxiety, worry, and sadness, and these feelings may be harder for him to dispel.

TEMPERAMENT AS GIFT

One's temperament is a gift from God that one should seek to understand and to accept. In our first two books, *The Temperament God Gave You* and *The Temperament God Gave Your Spouse*,[22] we describe in detail how understanding our temperament can help us know ourselves better, understand our spouse, motivate our children, and even grow in our spiritual lives. We are never "determined" by our temperament or forced to respond in a certain way. Our temperament is not our whole personality, nor does it put us in a box. Rather, it gives us important clues about our natural tendencies to react in certain ways, and this self-knowledge is an important step toward humility and Christian maturity. We should always seek to grow in wisdom and virtue. We may struggle to curb our tongue or reign in our temper. Or we may struggle to speak up when we would rather fade into the woodwork. We may struggle to contain our frequently changing emotions.

No temperament is better than or preferable to another—each has its own peculiar strengths and weaknesses. Temperaments are not moral weaknesses, simply tendencies that are not as strong as others. Many saints struggled to control (if not overcome) aspects of their own difficult temperaments. St. Vincent de Paul, for example, described himself as "naturally of a very bilious temperament and very subject to anger."[23] St. Jerome had a quick temper and easily got into arguments with others. He struggled all his life with his temper. In fact, it was because of his difficult temperament that he left Rome and went to the Holy Land. And that is where his greatest work—translating the Scriptures from Hebrew—took place. It can be comforting to know that God uses every aspect of our lives to build up his kingdom, as long as we humbly cooperate with him. Of course, St. Jerome also worked all his life to subdue his temper and to grow in virtue, and this helped him become a saint. Yet God calls each of us to become saints, and he doesn't require that we completely change our natural temperament. Grace never destroys nature but perfects it. Regardless of our natural tendencies, ultimately we will be "examined in love," as St. John of the Cross wrote.

TAKING AN HONEST
LOOK AT OURSELVES

Psychological and spiritual maturity require that we become aware of the ways in which our reactions are guided by our emotions—or sometimes misguided (as we will discover in the next chapter). Sometimes we may react purely on the basis of our emotions, yet our emotions may not be a sure guide. For example, our emotions may reflect a past inner wound, be the result of our temperament, or be due to our inordinately acquiescing to fluctuating moods. We need to recognize that we cannot blame our feelings on others or on external situations when instead, there is something in *me* (my temperamental bias) that gives rise to my anger or tears or frustration. I will be less likely to blame others, in fact, when I acknowledge honestly the weak links in my own temperament. When I take an honest look at my natural strengths and weaknesses, I will become not only more humble but also more willing to forgive those around me for their own faults.

Our temperament predisposes us to certain emotions. A sanguine tends to feel optimistic and happy, while a melancholic may tend to just the opposite; a choleric tends to react angrily to pressure, while a phlegmatic may feel anxious or fearful. These are simply tendencies and do not dictate our actions. When I reflect upon my natural inclination to certain emotional responses, I can decide to act in a different way. If I tend to be blithely optimistic, I can temper my natural reaction and be more prudent and cautious when the situation requires it. Or knowing that I have a tendency to respond aggressively, I will modify my instinctive reactions if the situation demands a more dispassionate approach.

We don't want to use our temperament as an excuse for bad behavior. I should not require my family and friends to adjust to my own moodiness or violent emotions. A mature Christian does not say, "I can't help it if I have a short fuse! Everyone else is just going to have to adjust!" or "Everyone needs to walk around on tiptoe around me because I am so sensitive!" (This attitude can be conveyed without words.) And if I already have a tendency to respond quickly or intensely (especially in anger), then I will be careful not to compound this reaction by overindulging in alcohol.[24] If I have a tendency to react pessimistically or to worry about future or past events, I can remind myself that some of my reaction is temperamentally based and does not necessarily reflect an accurate portrayal of the situation.

Christian maturity requires that we be honest and truthful with God, others, and ourselves—and it is often ourselves we most frequently deceive! Christian maturity—and truth—require that we examine our emotions carefully and determine (with our reason) whether they are reliable guides or not. In chapter 3, we will take a look at how we can identify when our emotions are helpful and when they might be hindrances.

So let's pause for a few moments to reflect on our own natural tendencies and give thanks to God for our natural strengths as well as for our weaknesses. This can help us grow in humility. We should neither *take* credit for our natural strengths nor *blame others* for their weaknesses, but rather, in everything give thanks to God, "who richly provides us with all things" (1 Timothy 6:17).

Going Further

1. What do you think your temperament is? Here is a quick summary: Are your emotions easily roused (choleric or sanguine)? Do you find yourself holding on to your feelings for a long time (choleric or melancholic)? Or do you easily let go of your strong emotions and easily forgive (sanguine or phlegmatic)? Are you slow to react, easy going, and rarely roused to anger (phlegmatic)? Or are you very sensitive and slow to respond, yet once the response sets in, you become more and more vehement over time (melancholic)? How does this knowledge help you understand your emotional reactions? How might it help you manage your emotions?

2. It is often said that opposites attract. If you are married, is your spouse opposite in temperament to you? For example, does he crave quiet and solitude while you love to talk and socialize? Or perhaps you are a perfectionist and she is rather sloppy. Does this sometimes give rise to conflict? How can an understanding of your spouse's temperament help you to grow in your marriage?

3. Many great figures of the Old and New Testaments—as well as many saints—had strong (some might even say "difficult") temperaments by nature. For example, Moses was quite irritable and easy angered (in a rage, he broke the tablets made by God himself!—Exodus 32:19). The "sons of thunder" (Mark 3:17), the disciples James and John, were so named for their fiery temperaments (Luke 9:54). St. Paul was "breathing murderous threats" against the disciples of Christ (Acts 9:1). And as a child, St. Thérèse of Lisieux had been stubborn, demanding, and moody. There are many more examples. God does not ask us to change our God-given temperament but rather, to grow in virtue and holiness. What might you do to help perfect your own nature? Is there a part of your nature that seems a little "rough around the edges"? Are you highly volatile, emotional, or easily angered? Or, on the other hand, are you afraid to reveal your deepest feelings? How can you become more well-rounded?

4. How can you grow in appreciation both for your own temperament and for those you love?

CHAPTER 3

CAN YOU TRUST YOUR FEELINGS?

*We must acknowledge the place which the heart
holds in the human person—a place equal in rank to
that of the will and intellect.*

—Dietrich von Hildebrand

W hat goes through our minds when we need to make a split-second decision? How do police officers and emergency responders make life-and-death decisions in mere milliseconds? What is the feeling we get in the pit of our stomach when we know that *something is wrong*? Can you know within minutes of meeting someone whether you like that person? Emotions provide "the first evaluation of events"; we feel sad, afraid, or happy even prior to conscious thought.[25] Then we think about what just happened and evaluate our feelings. In this way we make sense of our experiences. The fact that we can *reflect* on our immediate experience is precisely why we are greater than the animals. Even animals have feelings, but they do not reflect on them. Through the emotions a person "intuits the good and suspects evil" (CCC, 1771).

So our emotions play an important role in our ability to reflect on and evaluate our experiences. And while our faith has never denied the importance of the emotions, at times there has been a tendency to mistrust them. This mistrust perhaps stemmed from the Aristotelian position that the affective realm is "irrational," akin to that of the animals. Yet the fact that our emotions can sometimes lead us astray doesn't mean they are not valuable or helpful to us. As the philosopher Dietrich von Hildebrand writes, "There is no excuse for discrediting the affective sphere and the heart merely because these are exposed to so many perversions and deviations."[26]

Nonetheless, for these and other reasons, Catholics have, at times, emphasized the need to control, subjugate, and sometimes even repress feelings. Even today, some good Catholics fear strong feelings. Not too long ago, an article on a Catholic dating site advised young women to "never trust your heart" in matters of romance. But why should we never trust our hearts? Our emotions are a gift from God to help us discern what is good (or evil). It would be absurd to say to one's fiancée, "I rationally approached this relationship and determined that you meet all the criteria for an excellent spouse. I don't actually have any *feelings for you*, but I think you would make a good wife."

Very logical, Mr. Spock. But what kind of a marriage would that be?

When we love, we love with our whole being: body, mind, and soul. And this includes our feelings. Von Hildebrand discusses the crucial role of the heart in our spiritual lives. We may be tempted to be suspicious of our feelings because we know that sometimes we have experienced a superficial love or sorrow that didn't last. We may believe that since Christ has commanded us to love, and since we cannot force ourselves to feel love, then "true" love must be a matter of the will. Von Hildebrand points out that while this is true, still an act of reparation or doing our duty with a cold and unloving heart is certainly not a reflection of living a full Christian life.[27] Feelings such as happiness and consolation while praying, deep sorrow when confessing our sins, or exhilaration at sublime beauty are part of being fully human and open to the light of Christ that penetrates all aspects of our being. Part of becoming a mature Christian, then, is integrating in a healthy way our reason and our emotions, acknowledging our feelings while not letting them run amok or be taken over by sentimentality, histrionics, or perversions. St. Thomas Aquinas taught that at times when our passions cloud our reason, we end up making poor decisions, and that this is a product of original sin. Nonetheless, he also taught that our emotions are vital to growth in virtue. There can be no true courage without fear, and no true charity without love.

With the help of grace and reason, we can allow ourselves to feel deeply yet not be completely driven by our passions or victimized by irrational moods. If uncontrollable anger or fear seems to have a lock on our emotional lives, we may need to deal with past emotional wounds or trauma. How we can accomplish this is precisely our motivation for writing this book.

To Trust or Not to Trust?

We often mistrust our feelings because we view "negative" emotions like fear or anger as sinful. But as we noted earlier, feelings are morally neutral (CCC, 1767). They often arise in us spontaneously and are not deliberately willed. To the extent that they are not willful, they are not considered sinful.

Fr. Emmerich Vogt, OP, founder of the Twelve-Step Review, tells the story of a woman who goes to confession and repeatedly confesses her "dislike" of her daughter-in-law. He points out that even if he were to absolve her of what she thinks is a sin, it is highly unlikely that upon leaving the confessional, the woman would be suddenly overwhelmed by a fondness for her daughter-in-law. That is because her dislike is not voluntary. It is not an act of the will, which is a prerequisite for something to be considered sinful. But the woman should not act on the emotion by gossiping about her daughter-in-law or by being unloving or cruel. An emotion can become sinful when it is deliberately induced (such as deliberate hatred, which *is* a sin) or acted upon.

We can more easily trust in our feelings when we recognize that they are an integral part of our humanity and, as such, are important and valuable to our lives. "Feelings or passions are emotions . . . that incline us to act or not to act in regard to something felt or imagined to be good or evil" (CCC, 1763). When we spring out of the way of a swerving car, we are reacting appropriately to fear of an impending evil. When we read about social injustice, we are appropriately angry and protest that injustice. When we see the orphan in Haiti begging for food, we are filled with compassion and send money to a charity. When a loved one dies, we feel sad and weep. When we love, we are drawn to what or whom we love. If we did not experience such feelings, we would not be fully human. "Moral perfection consists in man's being moved to the good not by his will alone, but also by his sensitive appetite, as in the words of the psalm: 'My heart and flesh sing for joy to the living God' [Psalm 84:2]" (CCC, 1770).

In his bestselling book *Blink*, author Malcolm Gladwell shows that sometimes we do not trust in our feelings *enough*. He recounts the story of a ten-million-dollar statue purchased by the J. Paul

Getty Museum in the 1980s. Of course, the museum conducted extensive scientific tests to establish its authenticity. As soon as it went on display, however, a number of art experts instinctively felt that there was something wrong with the statue, even though they had viewed it only briefly. They couldn't pinpoint exactly what it was—it was only their *feeling* that something wasn't quite right that made them doubt its authenticity. Eventually, these feelings were confirmed: It was found to be a fraud. More than a year of study and scientific analyses had failed to reveal what the art experts had grasped in just a few seconds.[28]

Gladwell calls the making of a quick decision based on our gut feelings *thin slicing*. This sort of rapid cognition takes place in our unconscious, like a giant computer instantly sorting through all the data and coming up with a conclusion. It is the same kind of rapid decision making that happens when we see a big truck bearing down on us as we step into the street. We don't think through all our options consciously—we immediately jump out of the way. In one study, a psychologist had students rate college professors based on a mere two seconds of videotape. She compared the ratings with those of students who had actually studied with the same teachers for an entire semester. The ratings were essentially the same!

Thin slicing happens all the time. Usually people call this their "gut reaction" or "gut feeling." In fact, this is an example of the "intelligence" of emotions. If we were not hardwired to respond to our emotions, we might find it difficult to survive. Our emotion of fear helps us spring out of the way or prepares us to fight off an attacker. Our emotional bond with our children begins without our even thinking about it, as soon as the new baby is placed in our arms or even as soon as we feel new life stirring in the womb. Without even consciously making a decision, we "know" what to do: We avoid the danger, defend ourselves, or gather the newborn in our arms. Such is the "intelligence" of emotions—a gift of God.

FEELINGS HELP US MAKE DECISIONS

People who suffer brain damage that nullifies their emotional responses actually become unable to make decisions. Neurologist Antonio Damasio discovered that previously well-adapted individuals who had suffered damage to their ventromedial cortex could no longer identify what they *really wanted* to do in situations in which there was no clearly superior choice. These patients were completely rational and intelligent, yet became unable to make advantageous decisions about personal issues. For example, when asked to decide whether to schedule an appointment for Tuesday or Wednesday, one individual went back and forth for a half hour, listing reasons for and against each day. Ultimately, he simply couldn't decide—he had no emotionally based preference![29]

God has created us to be capable of experiencing strong feelings so that we can use them for good purpose. Neuroscientists have discovered that our brains are wired to respond empathically: When we hear a scream, we spring to action; when a baby cries, we immediately want to take care of it. Psychologist Daniel Goleman, author of *Social Intelligence*, says we are hardwired for compassion.[30] As the Catechism tells us, through our emotions we *intuit* the good and *suspect* evil. They are our God-given, built-in radar. Without them, we are stunted in our ability to make simple decisions about what is best for us. Growing in wisdom and in virtue means knowing when our feelings are leading us toward what is good for our soul, or when our feelings are disordered and leading us toward evil—and then making a prudent decision to follow what is truly good.

Our emotions provide us with the first intuitive evaluation of events and people in our lives—evaluations that are, as Malcolm Gladwell shows, often remarkably accurate. We thin slice whenever we need to quickly assess a new situation, meet someone for the first time, or make a quick decision.[31] As psychologist Leslie Greenberg puts it, this "integration of head and heart makes humans wiser than our intellects alone."[32]

Hitting the "Pause" Button

Nevertheless, we need to reflect on our emotions and decide whether to follow their urging or do something else. The rapid cognition offered by the emotional brain is not always precise or necessarily correct; therefore, we need to attend to and reflect on our feelings and our gut instincts. Our feeling of fear may be due to an impending danger (the truck bearing down on us), or it may be a nameless anxiety that wakes us up in the middle of the night in a cold sweat. Or consider that feeling of desire and love: It may not be appropriate if the object of my desire is someone else's spouse! Not every feeling needs to be acted upon. We must first reflect on and assess the situation.

This sort of reflection leads to self-knowledge and ultimately to better and more prudent decisions. For example, I may be an introvert and fearful of going to parties. But when I think about it,

I realize that I usually end up benefiting from social interactions. So I don't base my decision on my anxiety; I attend the party. Or I might have a short fuse and easily become angered when anyone interrupts me or contradicts me. But knowing this tendency, I make a conscious effort never to respond with angry words but to wait until I have counted to five or have calmly reflected on the situation.

Our thoughts (which we will discuss in chapter 5) and our feelings can lead us astray when they are not based on reality or truth—whether due to a past trauma, an unconscious set of faulty beliefs, or a bad habit of giving in to our passions. We have all had the experience of taking an instant dislike to someone we have just met. Sometimes further encounters prove our initial antipathy to be wrong. Sometimes these initial impressions are the result of unconscious prejudice. Author Stephen Covey tells the story of sitting on the subway with a father and his out-of-control children.[33] He judged the man to be an incompetent and derelict father—until he later learned that the man's wife (and the mother of the children) had just died. His snap judgment had been terribly wrong. Instincts (and unconscious prejudices) that are rooted in moral wrongs, such as racism, xenophobia, or deliberate hatred of our neighbor, lead us far from the love of God and neighbor.[34]

Similarly, only if our conscience is well formed can we can trust it. The Catechism reminds us that we have a God-given right to act in freedom, according to our conscience; however, our conscience must be properly educated and informed—which is a lifelong task (CCC, 1782–1783). "The lamp of the body is the eye. If your eye is sound, your whole body will be filled with light; but if your eye is bad, your whole body will be in darkness" (Matthew 6:22).

Here is an instance of trusting a gut feeling that is informed by years of experience and good judgment: A police officer sees a weapon being drawn on him, yet he makes a split-second decision to hold his fire until he can determine whether the assailant, who looks to be only fourteen years old, is truly dangerous or merely frightened. With the thinnest slice of information, he decides not to shoot, and the kid drops the gun.[35] Another example: A mother senses that something is wrong with her teenager. She acts on that gut feeling by having a talk with the child, who confesses that he has been indulging in alcohol or drugs. As Dr. Greenberg says, this integration of intellect and emotion makes us wiser than our intellects alone.

This point is echoed by the Catechism (1787–1788), which tells us that we must always seek what is right and good and try to discern God's will in our lives. To this end, we must *prudently interpret* the data of experience (for example, test our snap judgments and our first emotional response), seek wise advice, and pray for the help of the Holy Spirit.[36] The Holy Spirit works in us by "mobilizing the whole being, with all its sorrows, fears, and sadness" (CCC, 1769), as well as its desire, love, and joy, toward the ultimate good—the source of all goodness, God himself.

GOING FURTHER

1. In what ways do you appreciate the emotions God gave you? In what ways do they puzzle or confound you?

2. If you have a general mistrust of your emotions or the sense that you need to keep them under control or even repress them, how can you get into the habit of reflecting upon your feelings and deciding whether they are appropriate for the situation or not? What would help you to develop this habit?

3. Think about a time when your "gut feeling" helped you avoid a bad situation, identify a danger, or make a good decision. Why did you decide to pay attention to the feeling? Then think about a time when your gut feeling was way off base. What was the source of that feeling? What can this experience teach you about what to do in future situations?

4. The Catechism states: "Moral perfection consists in man's being moved to the good not by his will alone, but also by his sensitive appetite" (CCC, 1770). Why do you think that moral perfection involves not only the will but also the emotions?

5. How often have you confused an emotion with sin? How can you determine if an emotion is sinful or not?

CHAPTER 4

WHEN EMOTIONS ARE
OUT OF CONTROL

*Sometimes my feelings are so hot that I have
to take the pen and put them out on paper to keep them
from setting me afire inside.*

—Mark Twain

W e have all experienced days when our emotions seem
to be flying out of control. We may find ourselves
yelling at the kids, sulking over an insensitive comment, bursting into tears at the slightest provocation, or staying
up all night worrying.

Anger, sadness, fear, and anxiety—these are some of the
unpleasant emotions we experience. According to one research
study, people experience unpleasant emotions over pleasant ones
by a ratio of two to one.[37] Furthermore, our emotional reactions
can sometimes be quite complex since we can be experiencing several emotions at the same time. Once when our teenage son had
not returned from a date by midnight, Laraine became angry that
he hadn't called to let her know that he was running late; underlying this anger was the fear that he may have had an accident.

There are many reasons why our emotions can get out of control. For example, we may be tired, hungry, ill, or under intense
stress. But as soon as we eat, get rest, or finish that stressful project, we return to our usual disposition. Sometimes, however, we

experience unusual reactions that aren't explained by our immediate circumstances, or we continue to react in an over-the-top way despite our best efforts. Such reactions may be a reflection of a past emotional wound. Psychologist Paul Ekman relates a time when he overreacted to his wife's not calling him when she was out of town on a business trip. He experienced waves of anger, fear, and jealousy while waiting for her call—emotions triggered by his sensitivity to abandonment due to his mother's premature death when he was only fourteen years old.[38]

Even in the midst of an emotional outburst or an anxious meltdown, we may be aware that we *ought* to be responding differently—calmly and with self-control. We have a strong suspicion that we are overreacting, yet we give in to our emotions anyway. This is because it isn't really possible to "switch off" an emotion once it has started.[39] We can calmly reflect on the situation later, when we are not in the midst of the strong emotional reaction. We may then regret the feeling we had, the intensity with which we responded, or the angry or hateful things we said.

We may even be afraid of our own emotional intensity. It is common for men, especially, to fear their own anger. When people feel particularly overwhelmed by their emotional state, they may try to deny their emotions or ignore how they feel. If this becomes habitual, they may end up losing touch with their feelings. Alternatively, their fear of exploding may cause them to bottle up their emotions.

These are not healthy or effective ways to handle our emotions. Bottling up or suppressing our emotions is not wise because, as we discussed previously, our emotions have important information to give us—about the world, about other people, and about ourselves. Emotions are necessary to a healthy, full life, and a healthy emotional life contributes to our well-being and even our capacity to love and serve God and our neighbor joyfully and completely. Furthermore, bottling up emotions may lead to even greater explosions later on.

We need to better understand our emotional responses in order to take the first step in managing or regulating our emotions. The moments when we react inappropriately or in an emotionally out-of-control way may, in fact, tell us something important about ourselves.

We are not "ruled" by our emotions, as if we were puppets and our emotions were the puppet masters. Neither is it a matter of our being "in charge" of our emotions, as though we were tightly reigning in a bucking bronco. Rather, our emotions ought to mesh with the situation at hand. When our emotions are completely appropriate, we do not feel either manipulated by them or in charge of them.

For example, when we experience pride and joy as we watch our daughter winning a race, we do not regret or try to suppress our emotional response. Similarly, if we cry at a funeral or feel righteous anger when we see someone being mistreated, we find such a response perfectly appropriate. However, when we find ourselves yelling at the interruptive little toddler, waking up at night in anxiety, screaming at our spouse, or bursting into tears when a colleague makes a valid criticism, then we recognize that our emotions do seem to be controlling us. They are inappropriate to the occasion and somehow out of balance.

Is My Emotional Response Inappropriate?

St. Thomas Aquinas judged emotions or passions in terms of their appropriateness to the situation by asking whether the passion is "ordinate"—meaning as it "should be as to manner and time."[40] In other words, the emotion is neither excessive nor inadequate to the situation, and it does not last an excessive amount of time. For example, excessive anger or anger that turns into long-standing hatred would be considered inordinate.

But sometimes it's difficult to determine whether our own emotional responses are appropriate. One obvious way we can try to measure our emotional responses is by observing the reactions of other people. Are they tiptoeing around us because they are afraid that we will fly off the handle in a rage? Have we gotten into trouble for our bad temper? Do people consistently make unreasonable demands on us because we don't express our true feelings?

Another way to assess our emotional responses is to look at our activities objectively. Are we engaging in unhealthy activities such as overeating, viewing pornography, or spending hours in online chat rooms? Are we so sad that we can't get out of bed? Does our fear cause us to curtail our normal activities? Do we often get the same bad feelings, which leave us feeling paralyzed?

Some therapists recommend identifying our emotional responses as either "adaptive" or "maladaptive." If the emotional response is adaptive, it adds value to our life or creates a sense of well-being. If it is maladaptive, the emotional response is unhealthy, intense, and debilitating over time. A maladaptive response is a clue that something needs to be addressed. Here are some questions you can ask yourself to help you judge whether your emotional reaction was appropriate:

- Was my emotional response appropriate for the situation at hand? Did I overreact or underreact?
- Does this emotion help me respond correctly to the present situation, or does it get in the way?
- Does my response make me feel *more* out of control?
- Is something else bothering me such that I reacted so strongly on this occasion? Does this situation perhaps bring up uncomfortable feelings from my past?
- Does my emotional response signal correctly to others what I am feeling? Or are people confused by my expressions of emotion and feel pushed away?
- Am I generally able to regulate my emotions so that they are appropriate for the situation?
- Do I feel burdened and overwhelmed by my own emotions and moods? If I am sad, can others comfort me?
- Am I stymied in my emotions—either incapable of feeling or expressing them or incapable of deciding?

Assessing our emotions in this way helps us deal more rationally with them. The goal is to avoid the two extremes in dealing with emotions—either to completely suppress them or allow them complete sway. Neither is healthy. Rather, we can examine an emotional response and judge whether it is appropriate to the particular situation and helpful to us or not.

THE IMPORTANCE OF AWARENESS
AND REFLECTION

Managing our emotions instead of suppressing or ignoring them involves first becoming aware of our emotional reactions and then reflecting on them using our intellect and reason. This process helps us to learn about ourselves. For example, when Carl's boss makes a rather challenging remark about his work, he explodes in rage. His rage is an inappropriate response (especially in the work setting), leaving him with a feeling of being out of control and vulnerable in his job. He realizes he overreacted, and he reflects on the fact that he may have been reacting to long-buried feelings of anger toward his mother. His mother was controlling and manipulative, yet Carl never worked through his feelings of anger and fear. He recognizes that his feelings toward his mother were, perhaps, appropriate at the time but certainly inappropriate in the work setting. He learns what triggers his emotional hot buttons, and now he can take steps to prevent another inappropriate outburst.

In another example, Monica bursts into tears when her husband, Craig, comes home from work and says, "I'm starved! I didn't get lunch today because I was in one meeting after the other! What's for dinner?" Then she lashes out at Craig: "You have no idea how hard it is for me just trying to get the laundry done and the house picked up! How could I go to the store when the baby cried all day, and Joey was having a temper tantrum every time I tried to get him dressed?" Instantly she regrets her angry words and her over-the-top response.

Monica has been home all day with a toddler and a baby, feeling overwhelmed, disorganized, anxious, and resentful. The present situation—not having dinner ready, being frustrated with the kids, not having the house in order—has triggered anxiety from a painful childhood, with memories of chaos and disruption. Her response is inappropriate—maladaptive—because of her memory of her parents fighting when she was a child. Monica grew up feeling responsible for her parents' happiness: If she had been a "better," more cooperative child, maybe her parents would not have fought so often. In fact, the child Monica had not been responsible for her parents' behavior. But even now as an adult, she often feels that she ought to be "perfect" in order to make everyone happy. All this together has intensified the emotional response of the present, causing her to lash out in angry words to her husband.

Intense feelings of neglect or rejection (sometimes from a past traumatic experience) can be triggered by a present situation, giving rise to feelings that are not really appropriate at that moment. As we discussed in chapter 3, our feelings are often trustworthy in alerting us to what's important and what our needs are. They help us intuit what is good or evil and motivate us to take action against injustice or iniquity. Sometimes, as in the situations faced by Monica and Carl, our emotions give us a clue about something in our past that we should deal with. Perhaps Carl needs to let go of his anger and resentment toward his overbearing mother. Perhaps he can look back with forgiveness and compassion, realizing that his mom had struggled all her life with depression and anxiety. Monica can learn to let go of her need for perfection, and forgive herself when she is accomplishing less than her high standards would otherwise demand. Perhaps she can reframe her way of thinking: She is no longer a victim who is at the mercy of angry parents but a survivor of a tough childhood and a beloved child of God.

The process of awareness and reflection can also help us to learn about our loved ones. A couple came to counseling because they couldn't resolve a conflict about the husband's new job offer that involved relocating thousands of miles away. The husband was enthusiastic about the possibility of professional advancement, but the wife feared isolation and lack of support. Neither would listen to the other's feelings because each feared that this would indicate tacit approval of the spouse's position.

Art convinced the couple that empathy and understanding—really listening to one another—would not determine their ultimate course of action. He helped them express their own feelings and sincerely acknowledge the other's feelings without having to agree on an outcome. By acknowledging their mutual feelings and fostering an attitude of understanding and empathy, the couple was able to come to a decision that mutually benefited each spouse and took into consideration each of their deepest fears and anxieties.

OUR EMOTIONS LEAD TO ACTIONS

Our minds and bodies are meant for action.[41] The word "emotion" comes from the Latin word *emovere,* which means "to move or set into motion." The word "motivation" comes from *emovere* as well. Emotions can *"incline us to act or not to act in regard to something felt or imagined to be good or evil"* (CCC, 1763, emphasis added). Here is where we have to pay special attention, for our emotions are not always capable of analyzing the situation or being a prudent guide about what to do.

How to Act in Response to an Emotion

■ Emotions are reliable in moving us (*emovere*) to pay attention to some need, pain, or important aspect of ourselves or our relationships. For example, the fear that arises while walking down a dark alley rightfully compels me to get out of a dangerous spot. The compassion I feel for a lonely neighbor leads me to reach out to her in friendship.

■ Emotions give us intuitions about the next step, but they are not always reliable in guiding us in our action about what to do next. For example, when I am on a diet, my longing for food might impel me to take a piece of forbidden cake. My feeling of loneliness might move me to look at pornography. The feelings of hunger or loneliness are real and instructive as a self-assessment about myself, but I should think them through before responding.

■ Our reason is a better guide about what to do next because sometimes our emotions are taken up by sin or evil (CCC, 1768).

■ Sometimes our will or our intellect will tell us to just ignore our feelings. That may be appropriate (such as my nervousness about whether the front door is locked, even though I just checked it a few minutes before). Ignoring my feelings may also be wrong (I feel tired, but I'm going to keep on driving). In our most intimate relationships, ignoring our feelings can be perilous. And if I am feeling sad or upset, this might indicate that I need to talk with my spouse and reconnect.

For example, recently Art went to the retreat center near his office to check some messages. He walked past an old friend who was on a silent retreat. Since the man was on a silent retreat, he appropriately passed by Art without saying a word or even giving him eye contact. Art's first reaction was to *feel* rejected and ignored, and he was tempted to start thinking about why his friend would be so rude. He could have given in to resentment and might have been tempted to ignore his friend in their next encounter. But Art decided to reflect on the situation and try to look at it objectively. He realized that his friend was not rejecting him but trying to stay in the spirit of the silent retreat.

By reflecting on our emotional response, we can not only learn about ourselves and about life, but we can also have a better idea of how to act in the future. When Monica reflects on her over-the-top emotional response to her husband's request for dinner, she realizes that her rage was not appropriate to the situation but instead reflects her more complex feelings toward her parents. If she becomes aware of the triggers that might bring up these past issues, she will be less vulnerable when her husband makes an ill-timed request or insensitive comment. Monica might be proactive and greet her husband with a kiss at the door, saying, "You know, dear, I have had a really rough day, and I just didn't get to dinner. What do you think about ordering pizza tonight, and then both of us can relax?" Similarly, knowing his vulnerability to feelings of abandonment, Dr. Ekman shares that he should have prepared himself for the very realistic possibility that his wife would not call at the exact time he had expected. Had he prepared himself, he might not have reacted so intensely and angrily.

Our emotional responses are extremely complex. They often arise without our awareness, and often we can only describe or name the emotion we've experienced after the fact. Rather than suppressing, avoiding, or trying to control our feelings, a healthy approach is to experience the emotion and then review the situation. "A person has to have a healthy emotional life, for without it he is defenseless against the powers of evil," says Fr. Emmerich Vogt, OP.[42] Our intellect will tell us what is good and what is evil, but we can be so blinded by our inordinate passions that we no longer see the good. In this way, an unhealthy emotional life leads us astray.

When we learn to reflect rationally on our irrational moods and inappropriate emotional responses, we begin to break their tyrannical hold on us. Dietrich von Hildebrand writes:

When we overcome the despotism of these psychic feelings, we make room for spiritual feelings. . . . We can love what deserves to be loved, we can repent over our sins, we can experience the peace and light which the very fact of God's existence and of our redemption should bestow upon our soul.[43]

Take the time, alone or with the help of a spouse, spiritual director, or therapist, to reflect on what your emotions reveal about you and your relationships. Your God-given intelligence and reason will assist you in understanding—and possibly even transforming—your emotional responses.[44]

GOING FURTHER

1. When did you last feel emotionally out of control? Did you later take the time to reflect on your emotional response? If you do so now, using the questions above to assess your reaction, what insights do you come up with?

2. Is there an emotional wound from your past that sometimes governs how you react today? How can you best work through these wounds? Are you holding on to anger and resentment? How would forgiveness help?

3. Do you ever turn to unhealthy activities such as overeating or spending too much time Internet surfing or watching TV to distract you from your bad feelings? How can you better deal with these feelings?

4. In Matthew 7:5, Christ reminds us that we need to remove the plank from our own eye before we criticize others for their mistakes. We usually understand Christ to be cautioning us to recognize our own sinfulness before we worry about others' sinful behavior. But these planks in our eyes can also be prejudices, resentments, anger, unhealthy ways of thinking, or emotional wounds that prevent us from seeing our lives and our loved ones as they really are. In fact, a recent study showed that jealousy actually "blinds" people to the true situation.[45] As a result, we are less happy and joyful. What planks do you have in your own life? What issues are preventing you from living a spiritually and psychologically healthy life?

5. How might talking with your spouse, a spiritual director, or a trusted friend about your emotional reactions help you?

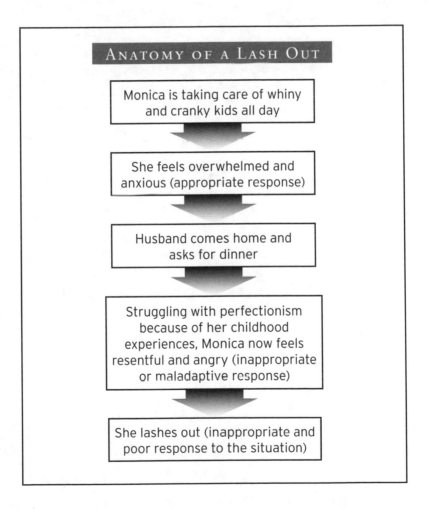

CHAPTER 5

HOW WE THINK AFFECTS HOW WE FEEL

When I was a child, I used to . . . think as a child.
—St. Paul (1 Corinthians 13:11)

Gary was feeling discouraged and unhappy with his life. He had recently been laid off. He knew the economy was in bad shape, but his area of the country had not been hit as hard as others. To make matters worse, among all his friends and acquaintances, he was the only one who had lost his job. He had saved up very little money, and when he looked at his résumé, it seemed pretty thin. "I feel like a loser," he thought.

As part of his unemployment benefits, Gary was given the opportunity to talk with a career counselor. The counselor asked Gary to recount what he was thinking whenever he filled out a job application or went to an interview. Gary sighed. "Every time I go into an interview, I think to myself, 'They're never going to hire me. I have little experience with all this new technology, and they won't want me. If they do, the job must be lousy.'"

This was a classic variation on the famous Groucho Marx routine: I don't want to join any club that would accept me as a member. Gary had gotten himself in a no-win frame of mind. If the interviewer actually seemed positive, he would think, "He won't like me when he gets to know me. I'm such a loser." If he didn't get a job offer, it only proved what he had suspected all along. Gary was paralyzed in every professional situation by his negative thoughts. His depressing thoughts ultimately made him feel . . . depressed.

We tend to think that our life experiences or what other people say or do make us feel good or bad. We think that situations determine our moods and our reactions. On the surface, it seems like a reasonable assumption: Gary is depressed because he lost his job. I am angry and frustrated because my kids are misbehaving or my husband works too many hours.

However, psychological studies show this assumption to be false. It turns out that one's circumstances in life, such as economic or health status, do not seriously affect one's happiness. A devastating accident, a serious illness, or unemployment can temporarily cause one to feel blue, but surprisingly, people typically bounce back to their previous state of happiness.[46] Even when faced with devastating loss, our feelings are uniquely our own and will differ from others. As Fr. Emmerich Vogt often says, "Happiness is an inside job."[47] How we feel depends on our interior state more than our exterior circumstances.

And—even more radical—how we feel sometimes depends on how we *think*.

Let's take another example. Art is presently on a diet. But one evening he simply can't resist a slice of apple pie. Immediately he feels frustrated and angry with himself. "I can never stick to a diet," he thinks. This is a single slip-up, yet he jumps to the conclusion that his diet will ultimately fail; now he feels discouraged and angry. Feeling discouraged makes him want to abandon the diet altogether. "There's no use," he thinks. How did this happen?

Could it be that his negative thoughts actually caused him to *feel* angry and frustrated?

Hasidic Rabbi Menachem Mendel used to say, "Think good, and it will be good." This sounds too simple, almost like magical thinking. But there is wisdom in this saying. Our thoughts (particularly our interpretation of events and circumstances), along with our temperament (our tendency to react in certain ways), will have a big (and possibly even greater) impact on our general mood than the situation itself.

Gary could have viewed the termination as a one-time unusual event that reflected more on the economy than on his own capabilities. With such views, Gary could have gone into each new interview feeling confident and optimistic. But instead, he went into each new interview feeling already defeated, and that feeling turned into a self-fulfilling prophecy. But where did that already-defeated feeling, or self-defeating train of thought, come from?

Bad Feelings Are Stronger Than Good Feelings

As we noted in the last chapter, we actually experience more negative emotions than positive ones.[48] To add insult to this injury, negative emotions are also *stronger* than positive ones. Bad thoughts, events, or feelings are stronger than good thoughts, events, or feelings. We remember bad events more vividly than good ones. The mean things people say hurt us deeply and are difficult to overcome; bad feelings are more intensely experienced and difficult to shake off.[49]

This helps explain why we tend to dwell on our mistakes and find it difficult to combat negative stereotypes. It's also why sad feelings linger after a misfortune and hurt feelings are difficult to shake. If your parents continually called you "lazy" when you were a child, you might have a hard time shaking that opinion of yourself even as a hardworking adult. Childhood wounds can have serious repercussions throughout a person's life. Even if you did not experience a trauma per se (such as a parent's death, a tragic accident, or abuse), certain experiences can leave a psychic "wound" that affects your emotional well-being in certain situations, especially situations that might trigger memories or attitudes from the past. (We discuss this in greater depth in chapter 8.)

As Gary and his counselor began exploring some of his self-defeating thoughts, he realized that ever since high school, he had labeled himself negatively. In the middle of his sophomore year, Gary's family had to relocate to a new city; he had to make new friends, and the new high school was far more rigorous academically. His grades dropped significantly; he became shy around his peers and withdrawn in the classroom. He began (almost unconsciously) to think of himself as a "loser"—even though he was not the cause of the situation in which he found himself. But even as an adult, when he began floundering, it triggered those past feelings of inadequacy and failure, and he immediately reverted to his teenage mind-set. His company's downsizing was a big challenge for him.

Gary came to realize that the way he thought as a child served as a coping mechanism during a particularly tough period of his life. As a teenager, he couldn't see himself asking for help from teachers and school counselors and stepping outside his comfort zone to make friends, so he (unconsciously) labeled himself as a "loser," thereby giving himself license to fail. Now, as an adult, this way of coping was no longer serving him and, in fact, it was hurting him. Gary found some comfort in the words of St. Paul: "When I was a child, I used to talk as a child, think as a child, and reason as a child" (1 Corinthians 13:11). It was time to change his old way of thinking. As Fr. Basil Maturin wrote in *Self Knowledge and Self Discipline*, it is "in light of our thoughts that we see and interpret the people and things around us. By a change of thoughts we change our view of life."[50]

A DISTORTED WORLDVIEW

In 1967 a psychiatrist named Aaron Beck developed a groundbreaking theory about the causes and treatment of certain psychological disorders such as depression and anxiety.[51] Beck had observed that his depressed patients often showed systematic distortions in their *thoughts*. They seemed to have a consistently negative view of themselves, the world, and the future. When the therapist asked them what they were thinking, they said things like "I'm sure I'm going to fail" or "I'm always overwhelmed" or "I can't handle this because I am so incompetent." They would systematically minimize positive experiences and overgeneralize or magnify negative ones. Their negative mind-set was actually causing them to feel depressed. In our simple example of Art's diet, his tendency to think "I can never stick to a diet" or "I am always overeating" causes him to feel frustrated, discouraged, and tempted to give up.

Dr. Beck's clients were feeling depressed not solely because of their current life situations but specifically because of the way they *interpreted* these situations: An unrealistic (or distorted) worldview can actually result in the individual's feeling bad and behaving in an unhealthy way. In other words, the person's thoughts were depressing him more than his actual situation.

Dr. Beck's cognitive-therapy model was shown to be helpful in treating depression, anxiety disorders, personality disorders, substance abuse, and many other problems. Much later Dr. Patrick Carnes showed that "faulty core beliefs" are a key factor in sexual addictions and lead some individuals to be more susceptible to such addictions.[52]

At the core of cognitive therapy is the assumption that our thoughts and feelings are significantly intertwined. We may believe we are thinking or behaving rationally, but many times we are not. In fact, when we are disturbed or upset, it is quite often the product of a faulty belief.

Of course, there are times when the disturbing or uncomfortable feeling is entirely appropriate—for example, feeling guilty when we have done something morally wrong. Feeling guilty is the correct response when we have committed sin, and our conscience rightly affects our emotions. In fact, we sometimes try to repress the voice of our conscience and rationalize our behavior through faulty beliefs: "My drug use doesn't hurt me; I can stop any time!" or "This extramarital affair will help my marriage!" or "My employer doesn't pay me enough; I deserve to skim some money off the top." Such faulty thinking will lead to further inappropriate feelings such as lust and a desire for ill-gotten money, which are encouraged by the faulty reasoning that seeks to justify sinfulness and sinful habits.

WHAT WAS I THINKING?

Try this sometime when you find yourself experiencing a sudden and overwhelming bad mood or sadness: Ask yourself, "What was I just thinking?" Perhaps you were just beginning a new class, and you looked at the reading list and said to yourself, "I'll never be able to keep up! This reading list is way above my skill set." Then you felt a huge weight on your shoulders, a feeling of despondency and helplessness. Or you looked at your budget and thought to yourself, "It's no use even trying to stick to a budget. I'll never make enough money to pay all these bills. It's hopeless." You then felt sad and discouraged. Or you left the job interview realizing that out of fear, you failed to discuss your strengths. You said to yourself, "I wouldn't have gotten that job anyway. I'm not qualified."

We can pause and take note of such thoughts, possibly jotting them down over a week's time. When you experience a negative emotion, ask yourself, "What was going through my mind just then? What did this situation remind me of?" Once you recognize the thoughts you had that generated the emotion, you can begin to slowly unpack the belief system or core beliefs that underlie these negative recurring thoughts. The core beliefs might be something like "People always let me down" or "I'm never going to find someone to love" or "I am not very smart" or "I never succeed at anything."

Gary's thoughts were causing not only occupational problems (he tended to be passive at work and frequently put himself down) but also social problems (he was afraid to take chances and was unassertive). It turned out that underlying some of Gary's negative feelings was a set of core beliefs about himself, others, and the world. These automatic negative thoughts (or core beliefs) are sometimes called "schema" because they form a set of beliefs that we seem to return to over and over again and that may solidify into a worldview that colors our responses. These core beliefs tend to be activated during times of stress when we are embarking on new experiences or in other life situations. Without our even realizing it, our schema may cause us to misread the objective facts of the situation, usually in a negative way. Furthermore, these thoughts can affect how we feel.

Self-Defeating Core Beliefs

Gary's negative core beliefs were often triggered in times of severe stress, and Gary himself was not even consciously aware of them until he began examining his thoughts more carefully. Underlying his anxiety and depression were thoughts such as "I am inadequate and incapable of success" or "Other people are smarter than I am, more deserving and capable" or "The world is unpredictable, demanding, and scary." Prompted by his counselor, Gary started to pay attention to his thoughts and began to realize that highly critical and self-defeating thoughts would automatically arise in stressful situations such as a job interview, asking someone out on a date, or undertaking a challenging new project.

Many of us have similar underlying core beliefs. When faced with certain situations, especially those that are stressful, our schema can be activated. Instead of living in the present moment and facing each situation as a new one, we immediately return to the pattern of coping that we are most familiar with; for many, this is a pattern of negative, self-defeating thoughts. Instead, we need to challenge our old habitual way of thinking—especially if it is undermining our psychological or spiritual health. In order to feel different, we need to learn to think differently. But when our schema are especially ingrained or nearly "unconscious," it can be difficult to change!

Gary's counselor wrote down the negative thoughts that Gary told him would pop into his head unbidden. He asked Gary if these statements were true. "Is it really true that you are incompetent and unemployable?" he asked. "What's the worst thing that could happen if you asked that woman out on a date?" Gary learned to remind himself of the successful things that he had done and how he was a good friend and a diligent employee.

Gary finally realized that his thoughts were related to an unhealthy schema formed when he was a teenager and that these negative ways of thinking no longer applied. They were a child's response to a very difficult situation, and certainly now that he was an adult, he could retrain his thinking. This realization helped him make the commitment to get rid of such negative thought patterns; he needed to stop the automatic thoughts from rushing in whenever he was under stress. After Gary had discovered some of the faulty beliefs that were undermining his interviews and limiting his social prospects, he began learning how to decrease (and even nullify) the impact of such thoughts.

SUBMIT EVERYTHING TO THE
LIGHT OF REASON

We need to recognize when self-defeating thoughts automatically rush in and take over, highjacking our moods and our lives. The key is to recognize the discouraging thoughts, as well as the situations that trigger them, and replace them with more accurate and supportive thoughts. Because such thoughts often arise unbidden in our unconsciousness, they need to be examined with the light of reason.

Of course, not all uncomfortable feelings and negative thoughts are faulty or irrational. For example, guilt after committing a sin, remorse after a moral failure, or anxiety and fear about doing something impulsive or unwise are all entirely appropriate feelings and help motivate us to do the right thing. Our conscience will often nudge us in the right direction through appropriate spiritual feelings such as remorse and sorrow.

That is why we need to put our thoughts to the test and examine our feelings with the light of reason. If you are struggling with unhealthy and self-defeating thoughts, you want to eliminate them. But as Jesus told us in the parable of the unclean spirit, you don't want to leave your house (or your mind) empty so that more unclean spirits can return (Luke 11:24-26). Recognize the self-defeating thoughts, and replace them with good thoughts—the way God sees you—and with his plan for your life. As Fr. Maturin explains, "The effort of the soul must be to fill the mind so full of healthy thoughts that there is no room for others—trying not so much not to think of what is evil as to think of what is good."[53]

We are not suggesting that you become a mindless Pollyanna, thinking only "happy thoughts," since this is not a mature Christian attitude. Nor can you banish everything negative through strength of will alone, since this is not likely to work. The point that Fr. Maturin is trying to make is that evil needs to be overcome with good. For example, people who want to quit smoking need to take up another hobby that is incompatible with smoking but (hopefully) equally compelling, such as running. If I am in a despondent mood, instead of sulking around morosely, I should do something positive and worthwhile—visit a sick relative, do a good deed, take a vigorous walk, make a visit to the Blessed Sacrament chapel. Or if I am angry, instead of feeding my anger by dwelling on the rank injustice of my situation or past grievances, I can turn my thoughts to something more constructive and pray for those who have offended me. Fr. Maturin writes:

> He therefore who would overcome any habit of evil thoughts must do so indirectly rather than directly, trying not so much not to indulge in anger as to fill the mind with loving and kindly thoughts, meeting discontent by rejoicing in the will of God, self-consciousness by wrapping oneself round in the Presence of God—turning as promptly as possible to think of something bracing when one is conscious of the presence or approach of evil.[54]

In prayer, with frequent reception of the sacraments (and, if necessary, with the help of a professional counselor), we can remind ourselves that we are loved unconditionally by God. Thoughts of our own inadequacies and failings may fill us with shame, and the devil may tempt us to despair and to think we are unlovable or hopeless. We must push such thoughts away, turn to God in fervent prayer, and throw ourselves into the arms of the Blessed Mother. We can seek to live "with the mind of Christ" (CCC, 2046) by reflecting on the Scriptures, especially reflecting on God's saving and healing power. In this way, we can replace the negative and false thoughts by the truth that we are beloved children of God. As the prologue to the Catechism says, "God, infinitely perfect and blessed in himself, in a plan of sheer goodness freely created man to make him share in his own blessed life" (I, 1). God so loved each one of us that he gave his only Son (John 3:16), and he continues to call each one of us to friendship and happiness with him.

PUT YOUR THOUGHTS TO THE TEST

Here is a step-by-step way to put your thoughts to the test:

1. Identify situations in which your emotional response is inappropriate and reactive. For example, an acquaintance doesn't acknowledge your presence at a party, and you feel upset for hours. Or your boss makes a critical comment about one of your proposals, and you feel angry and discouraged for days.

2. Identify what you were thinking at the time you were experiencing such feelings. For example, when you were at the party and you saw the friend who apparently ignored you, did you think to yourself, "I am being rejected" or "Nobody really likes me!" or "People never find me interesting." Or regarding the

example about work, did you think, "Nobody ever appreciates the work I do!" or "I'm such an underachiever."

3. Reflect on how such thoughts impact your mood. Did you slip into a blue funk after you began thinking how you are always being ignored? Or did you become angry when you started thinking that your boss never appreciates you?

4. Reflect on whether you often have such thoughts in other situations and how these thoughts affect how you see yourself: "Is this how I understand myself and feed a feeling of rejection?" Begin to recognize the triggers (for example, stressful situations, new situations, changes in routine, being sick or extremely tired or hormonal, spending time with your parents or in-laws, and so forth).

5. Test the validity of your thoughts. Dr. Philip Scrofani, a professor and director of clinical training at the Institute for the Psychological Sciences, recommends "Socratic questioning" to bring rational reasoning to emotionally vulnerable situations. Questions you should ask include the following:

- What is the evidence for this thought?
- Is there an alternative explanation?
- What is the worst that can happen?
- What is the most realistic outcome?
- What is the impact of believing this?
- How would I advise a friend who was thinking this way or had this problem?

For example, does it follow that I am boring or a loser or unlovable because somebody didn't say hello to me at a party? Did he actually intend to ignore me? Perhaps he wasn't wearing his glasses. If a friend told me about this incident, I would tell him that most likely his acquaintance had simply not seen him and had never intended to slight him.

How we think affects our feelings and can affect our self-appraisal. Sometimes our governing thoughts are irrational, overly negative, or a habitual way of thinking from childhood that no longer applies. Such thoughts can hamper our ability to live a rich, healthy life and respond freely to God's call. We need to submit our irrational thoughts or faulty core beliefs to the light of reason and be guided by the truth instead of our fears. No longer shackled by the chains of negativity and false thoughts, we are free to respond to God's grace and to embrace new habits of doing good.

GOING FURTHER

1. According to the Catechism, "It belongs to the perfection of the moral or human good that the passions be governed by reason" (1767). We typically associate "reason" with "thinking," but in this chapter we have shown that sometimes our thoughts are not rational or reasonable. How often are you subject to thoughts that are unreasonable? What are some clues that could tip you off to the fact that your thoughts aren't reflecting reality or the truth of the situation?

2. Are there any underlying core beliefs that you inadvertently assent to, especially in times of uncertainty or stress? Give some examples from your life in which you may have overreacted to a spouse or co-worker's comment, indulged in unhealthy behavior, or otherwise reacted inappropriately. What might have been the unhealthy automatic thoughts that influenced your feelings?

3. Lustful, hateful, or vengeful thoughts can also fuel our emotions. How can the sacraments—in particular, the Sacrament of Reconciliation—help you to fight such thoughts? How might the truth of Scripture help?

4. Can you recall a situation in which a faulty belief or a set of irrational thoughts hurt your spiritual life? What were these thoughts? What thoughts and attitudes did you replace them with? Were your prayer and sacramental life instrumental in turning things around?

CHAPTER 6

WHAT WE DO AFFECTS HOW WE FEEL

When I do good, I feel good.

—Abraham Lincoln

What makes us happy? As we discovered in chapter 2, our natural disposition plays a critical role in our emotional life. Our temperament directly affects the frequency and intensity of our emotions as well as our tendency to have certain moods.[55] Research studies have shown that our genetic makeup (which includes temperament) contributes up to 50 percent of a person's overall "happiness quotient"—whether one tends to look on the bright side or is prone to sadness.[56]

Typically we think life *circumstances* affect our general outlook. But as we discussed in the last chapter, psychologists have found that the overall feeling of well-being of individuals who were in unfortunate circumstances was not significantly altered in the long run by those circumstances. Similarly, those who won the lottery, bought a new house, or got married had a brief upswing in happiness but then returned to the same emotional state they had before these things happened. We might think that our level of happiness would depend on our education, age, or income level, but in fact, only about 10 percent of our emotional well-being is due to life circumstances![57]

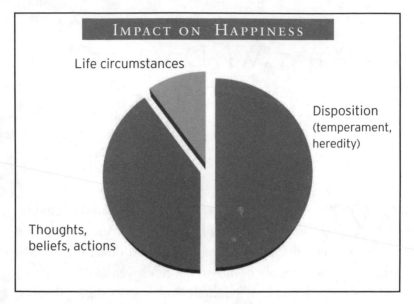

IMPACT ON HAPPINESS

Life circumstances

Disposition (temperament, heredity)

Thoughts, beliefs, actions

If 50 percent of our "happiness quotient" is due to temperament and other biological factors (disposition)and 10 percent is due to life circumstances, what accounts for the other 40 percent? If we tend to be somewhat pessimistic by nature, is there something we can do to become happier? The answer is a resounding yes.

Research has shown that what we *do* is highly significant. What we do—our attitudes and our behavior—can actually influence how we feel.

Psychologist Paul Ekman, author of *Emotions Revealed*, has studied emotions for more than forty years. (In fact, the TV show *Lie to Me* was based on his research of reading facial expressions to identify lying behavior.) Ekman found that making certain facial expressions triggers changes in our bodies and brains.[58] So making a sad face can trigger unhappy memories and "putting on a happy face" can actually lift our spirits. More significant, the way we behave can have a positive impact on our emotional lives.

Psychologist Martin Seligman has spent many years studying the science of happiness. The founder of Positive Psychology, he wanted to change the focus of psychology from always being about what is broken (dysfunction and mental illness) to what helps human beings rise to higher levels of well-being. What makes us feel happy, hopeful, and productive? What gives meaning and energy to our lives? In his many studies on optimism, virtue, and happiness, he has found that there are some things we can do to improve our emotional well-being.

Faith, family, and friends contribute significantly to our overall sense of happiness and well-being. People who have strong interpersonal connections and social support have the highest levels of happiness and the fewest signs of depression. Many studies have confirmed the fact that married people are healthier and live longer than unmarried people.[59] How do strong interpersonal connections and social support contribute to happiness, wellness, and well-being?

Happiness Is Other People

Unhappiness is often a product of feeling insecure, threatened, distressed, or abandoned. Victims of trauma often suffer feelings of helplessness or rage. When people lack the physical or emotional support of strong interpersonal connections, they are especially vulnerable and have difficulty regulating their emotions, which can range from feeling numb to being overwhelmed by negative emotions.[60] Strong, healthy relationships can actually have a healing and transformational effect on those who have suffered trauma in the past. This makes sense because fundamentally, we are relational beings.

When God created the heavens and the earth and man in his image (Genesis 1:27), he deemed everything good—except for one thing: "It is not good for the man to be alone" (2:18). When discussing the Book of Genesis in his famous Wednesday catechetical instruction that became the "theology of the body," the late Pope John Paul II wrote: "The unity which is realized through the body ['and the two shall become one'] indicates, right from the beginning, . . . the incarnate communion of persons."[61] In fact, in this community of persons, man becomes the image of the Trinity—relational in its very nature.

We, too, are meant to be in relation with God and others. Our personal relationship with Christ can carry us through many storms and crises of life and will strengthen our relationships with others. He calls us to himself: "Come to me, all you who labor and are burdened, and I will give you rest" (Matthew 11:28). When we draw closer to Christ and allow him to carry our burdens, we find peace and rest amid the difficult circumstances and the turmoil of life. Our relationships give us a secure base from which we can take chances in our journey through life so that we become more trusting and self-giving. Our loving relationships with Christ and others help us handle the inevitable struggles, setbacks, and sorrows of life. When love is foundational, we can withstand the storms of emotions like sadness, anxiety, and fear.

THE IMPORTANCE OF GRATITUDE

In his research, Seligman also found that we can increase our happiness by being thankful, performing acts of kindness, and taking the time each day to write down three things that went well. When we consciously choose to be grateful, even in difficult circumstances, our ability to see the good in life is strengthened. With time and practice, "seeing your cup half full" can become a mental habit. On the other hand, a sense of entitlement blocks gratitude. When our attitude is that we are being shortchanged in life or that we somehow got a "raw deal," we create for ourselves a state of constant dissatisfaction and unhappiness.

According to St. Thomas Aquinas, there are three important aspects to gratitude:

1. *To recognize* the favor received.
2. To *express* one's appreciation and thanks (acknowledge).
3. *To repay* the favor at a suitable place and time according to one's means.

Seligman found that the greatest boost to our joy was caused by what he called the "gratitude visit." This involves writing a note in which we express our gratitude to someone who has helped us, and then visit that person and read the letter to him or her.[62] This gratitude visit embodies all three important aspects of the virtue of gratitude as outlined by St. Thomas. It may seem "over the top" to write—and read—a letter of gratitude to someone who has helped us; however, the key point here is that *overt* gratitude increases our joy. So often we think that friends and family members just "know" that we love and appreciate them—as though by osmosis. In fact, we need to be over-the-top in our expressions of love and gratitude—through our words and our actions.

THE HAPPY MORAL LIFE

The view that our behavior influences our emotional well-being jibes with Catholic theology and is further evidence of the psychological benefits of Christian charity—not to mention the benefits in terms of our eternal salvation! Doing good and being virtuous ultimately should contribute to our happiness, both in this life and the next. Living a good and morally responsible life makes us feel better about ourselves and our world. Living a life of sin or becoming a slave to our passions makes us feel bad about ourselves and ultimately puts our salvation on the line: "For the wages of sin is death" (Romans 6:23).

A responsible, happy, and fulfilling life *is* the morally good life.[63] The healthier, happier individual is usually one who makes good choices, is virtuous, and has a certain degree of self-knowledge and self-mastery. The Catholic view is that through good moral decisions and self-mastery, one is increasingly happy. Our relationship with Christ gives us the grace to make those good moral decisions and the strength to grow in virtue. By nature, every person wants to be happy. Nobody sets out to choose what is evil. However, we can be misguided or deceived as to what actually is good for us. We can be swayed by our passions to choose something detrimental to our overall health and happiness.

To use a simple example, I *really* want to eat that piece of chocolate cake. But I shouldn't because I am ten pounds overweight and my goal is to lose a few pounds and become healthier. So I refrain from that pleasurable experience of eating the cake, and thereby practice virtue. Initially, I might have thought that I would be "happy" if I could just have one slice of chocolate decadence. In fact, I am happier by achieving self-mastery and my goal to lose weight. Ultimately, giving in to my passions does not make me a happy person. I experience a greater joy in being virtuous—in eating right, being healthy, and making wise choices. Subsequently, I will realize that I have a greater sense of satisfaction and a greater sense of freedom than when I was self-indulgent.

WHAT IS VIRTUE?

St. Thomas Aquinas, considered the master theologian on virtue, defines virtue as the habit (something that is readily or easily done) of doing good.[64] Aquinas appropriated the Greek philosopher Aristotle's view that virtue is the mean between excess and defect—it is the "golden mean." The virtuous act is one that is neither excessive nor deficient. So, for example, courage is neither foolhardy nor cowardly, and temperance is neither total abstinence nor gluttony. Humility is neither arrogance nor subservience. Perseverance is neither obstinacy nor capitulation.

One might also understand this "golden mean" as balancing our desires with reason. To use the example of the soldier in the first chapter, he was afraid (perhaps his instincts were to flee), yet he balanced his instinct or desire to flee with reason (he knew that the right choice would be to remain at his post). Through his training, the soldier developed the *habit* (virtue) of following reasonable orders. Virtue helps us attain our goals—in this case, the goal of protecting his post.

St. Thomas understood the importance of emotions in relation to virtue. Virtue is not incompatible with emotion as long as the emotion is subject to reason. In fact, he even concluded that each cardinal virtue (prudence, temperance, justice, and fortitude) *requires* ordinate (reasonable) emotion.[65]

The key is that the emotions, in order to contribute to virtue, must be subject to reason. As we discussed in chapter 4, emotions should be neither inordinate nor maladaptive; they should be appropriate to the situation. Regulating our passions by subjecting our emotions to the light of reason helps us to maintain a well-balanced approach in the face of life's inevitable struggles. Practicing self-restraint and growing in virtue (the habit of doing good) help us become happier and more productive members of society.

We will not have this sense of accomplishment and self-mastery if we are forever giving up on our tasks or if we are slaves to our passions. Nor will we feel a sense of purpose and meaning as long as we are tortured by self-doubt, driven by fear, on an emotional roller coaster, or driving people away because of our unbalanced emotions and out-of-control passions. A truly mature person is one who knows himself—his own strengths and weaknesses—and who has grown in virtue and self-giving.

But what if we aren't there yet?

Virtue and the State of
Our Emotional Health

According to some psychologists, a well-balanced emotional life may be a prerequisite for growth in virtue. Deep emotional wounds or a lack of self-acceptance (if one considers oneself unlovable, for example) can hinder our sense of being lovable, and can even hurt our ability to freely choose the good.[66] Consider the classic story of the teenage girl who feels rejected by her dad so she runs off with the first boy that shows her some attention.[67] Or consider the young man who can't hold a job because he is continually rebelling against all authority figures—even as an adult. There are many who struggle with same-sex attraction because of emotional wounds as children. Healing deep emotional wounds is often the first step in becoming more capable of growth and of making rational, objectively wise choices.

Someone who was abandoned or physically abused as a child might have a difficult time being open to love and might have a tough time choosing healthy relationships. (In chapter 8 we discuss emotional wounds and trauma in more depth.) A past trauma or a serious emotional wound can have a serious impact on a person's ability to trust and to form intimate relationships, especially if the trauma involved the betrayal of trust by a loved one. This makes it difficult to trust others with our deepest thoughts and most intimate feelings and to trust that we will not be abandoned or hurt again. But if new, responsive, and trust-building relationships are established, it will ease the wounds of the past and help the person to see himself or herself differently (and more positively), allowing for more healthy emotional responses and growth in virtue.

When we are bound up by fear and anxiety or we are feeling depressed, we find it very difficult to do anything, much less something good. Extreme emotions can paralyze us. Someone who is depressed no longer feels any joy in life—not even about things that he or she knows are wonderful. The depressed person may be too exhausted to get out of bed, even for a cup of steaming hot coffee. Another person may be so fearful and anxious that she can't seem to make a simple decision.

Moods can be nearly as stultifying. A mood lasts much longer than a specific emotion—sometimes hours, days, or even months. A mood narrows our emotional options. If we are in a "blue mood," we are predisposed to becoming sad; if we are in a grumpy mood, we are ready to become angry at the slightest provocation. If we are in a good mood, we are less likely to become provoked by troublesome situations. In most cases, when we are in a mood, we are less likely to read the situation objectively and more likely to respond inappropriately. Yet a mood lacks a specific object or target, and sometimes does not even have a clear cause. We really can't say *why* we are in a bad mood, a good mood, or an irritable mood.[68]

As long as the mood is not debilitating or dangerous (requiring professional help), we can take a look at our moods rationally: Is there any reason for me to be in this mood? If not, try some creative ways to snap out of it: get some exercise, take a walk outdoors, make a visit to the chapel, spend time in prayer, perform an act of gratitude or compassion, or in some way get outside yourself to help others who are less fortunate.

Ultimately, to feel a sense of satisfaction about our lives and to feel well-balanced and happy, we need to experience and believe in God's love for us personally. God has a plan for each of us, and we need to feel that we are significant, that we have an ultimate purpose in our life, and that we are appreciated and loved by God and by others. God wants to heal us of anything that prevents us from experiencing his love and mercy. As we open ourselves more to God's love and presence in the sacraments and the Scriptures, we will come to understand that God loves and accepts us and wants to accompany us on our life's journey. He wants to take on our burdens (Matthew 11:28) and share the crosses of life with us, bringing us his rest, peace, and joy.

VIRTUOUS AND UNHAPPY?

As we explained earlier, virtue is usually understood as the habit of doing good; doing good becomes part of one's disposition or character through repeated good acts. This, in turn, shapes an individual's inclinations so that they are ever more inclined to the good. And as we increase our ability to make good choices and grow in virtue, we find a corresponding increase in our emotional well-being. As the famous saying goes, "Virtue is its own reward."

However, doing good and virtuous acts does not *always* cause us to feel happy. If we are performing virtuous acts solely as a matter of duty, because we "ought" to do so, we may not feel a corresponding sense of *joy* in doing good. We also risk becoming overbearing, self-righteous, and critical of ourselves and others. There may be underlying reasons why being virtuous does not lead to a sense of joy in accomplishment.

Psychologist Frank Moncher and theologian Craig Titus describe a case study of a religious sister, a consecrated member of a Catholic religious congregation.[69] Sr. Lydia (a pseudonym) was a dutiful and hardworking member of her community, but she was feeling exhausted in her daily routine, and she kept herself emotionally distant from her sisters in the community.

The authors explain that Sr. Lydia was doing the right things externally, yet she felt no corresponding joy or pleasure in them. It was like a stoical "white knuckling" that doesn't have the happy result of freely and easily choosing the good and feeling a corresponding joy. It turns out that Sr. Lydia had been stuffing her feelings for a long time because of deep emotional wounds from her childhood. She kept herself distant from her sisters in the community because she had learned (from childhood) that other people (even loved ones) were untrustworthy and potentially dangerous. She needed to become aware of how her childhood situation was affecting the way she related to her fellow sisters in her community. Because she was always afraid that her emotions would erupt inappropriately, she withdrew from her fellow religious and repressed her own feelings.

Sometimes very well-intentioned Catholics (perhaps Sr. Lydia) fear that emotions in themselves are evil, and so it's better to bottle them up than to express them. But as we discussed in chapter 1, evil doesn't lie in our passions, our intellect, or our will. It does not lie in our faculties but rather in the object of our desires or will. So we don't have to be afraid of our emotions. God wants us to turn the power of our passions and our will toward that which is truly good

Sr. Lydia's case does not necessarily detract from the valid point that doing good does make us feel better—especially when we are truly acting virtuously. But being happy or feeling joy in our virtuous actions may not occur immediately. In those times, we need perseverance and patience. The first week I am working out at the gym, I may feel sore and exhausted; I might even feel frustrated, but if I keep going, I will see benefits to my health. If I am taking care of an elderly parent, I may not feel a sense of continual joy or immediate happiness in my caretaking role. But when I look back on the situation, perhaps after that person has passed away, I will know that I did my best to love and care for him, and I will be filled with peace rather than with regrets or guilt.

WE NEED PRACTICE

Imagine trying to play a musical instrument with no knowledge of how to do so. The sounds emitted from the instrument will be terrible and painful to the ear. But once you have struggled through learning the notes and how to follow the rules (which is tedious and requires self-discipline), you will be able to play beautiful music. After all those hours of practice, the beautiful music is your reward.

Growing in virtue is similar. Like practicing in order to play a musical instrument well, the road to happiness requires self-control and perseverance. Through education, the deliberate performance of virtuous acts, and perseverance, we can grow in the human virtues (as opposed to the theological virtues of faith, hope, and charity, which are infused by God into our souls). As we continue our musical practice, our options improve. We are no longer limited to simple tunes like "Chopsticks"; we can now play music by Chopin and Beethoven and Debussy. We are happier as we become more accomplished. Similarly, practicing virtuous acts helps us grow further in virtue, improves our character and our relationships, and even brings us happiness. As the Catechism bluntly states: "Either man governs his passions and finds peace, or he lets himself be dominated by them and becomes unhappy" (2339).

With growth in virtue and self-mastery, both freedom and happiness increase. Of course, a "white knuckling" attempt to be virtuous without surrendering to a relationship with Christ can end up in stoic self-righteousness that fails to achieve the true good that a virtuous life intends. But through God's grace, our human virtues will become infused with love for God and will be directed toward him. Then, as St. Paul wrote to the Romans, "All things work for good for those who love God" (Romans 8:28).

GOING FURTHER

1. Do your relationships provide a sense of security and stability in your life? What can you do specifically to nurture your relationships and grow in intimacy and trust with the ones you love? How might this help you emotionally?

2. St. Paul understood the importance of gratitude, and he emphasized it many times in his letters. He knew that a grateful heart engenders joy. He wrote to the Philippians: "Rejoice in the Lord always. I shall say it again, rejoice! Your kindness should be known to all" (4:4-5). Paul tells the Colossians that they should walk in the Lord "abounding in thanksgiving" (2:7). There are many other instances in his letters when he expresses abundant gratitude to both God and to his fellow Christians.[70]

Think about a specific aspect of your life in which you are particularly blessed. Does this raise your spirits? What are some ways you can express your gratitude—to God, to your spouse, to your children, to your friends and family? How might this improve your relationships?

3. Make a list of the things that you do regularly that bring you the most joy and happiness, not just for the moment, but for a long time. Are they things that involve virtue and acting charitably and justly? What else might you do to increase your happiness?

4. How does your experience of God's love affect the way you feel about yourself? What could you do on a regular basis that might help you feel God's love for you (such as attending daily Mass, going to confession, praying with Scripture, or caring for the poor)?

5. Sometimes we judge an action to be virtuous when it is not. For example, Fr. Emmerich Vogt tells the story of a woman who was sweeping the floor when her critical and overcontrolling husband said, "You missed a spot." At first glance, one might think the woman was being virtuous by humbly and obediently sweeping that spot she missed. However, the truly virtuous act would have been to confront her controlling spouse and say, "Here's the broom. You can get it. It's good enough for me." By speaking out, both she and her husband would have had the opportunity to grow in virtue. The truly virtuous path is neither arrogance nor false humility.

Similarly, if I fail to confront an alcoholic spouse, I am not being charitable, I am being codependent. Is there an area in your life in which you think you are acting virtuously but in the long run may not be? Talk to a trusted friend or spiritual director about the situation and what you might want to do to change your response.

6. Dr. Seligman's suggestion to write a letter of gratitude to someone and then to read it to him or her in person may seem a bit over-the-top and inconvenient. What are some ordinary ways that you can more overtly express the appreciation and gratitude you feel toward your friends, family members, and co-workers?

CHAPTER 7

DEALING WITH ANGER

*Give up your anger, abandon your wrath; / do not be
provoked; it brings only harm.*

—Psalm 37:8

Have you ever been so angry that you literally "saw red"?
Or so resentful that whenever you thought about a
certain incident or person, you became angry all over
again? Have you ever thrown something in anger or even hit
someone? Or perhaps you have lived with an angry person and
were constantly tiptoeing around on eggshells lest the "simmering
volcano" explode. Anger is a powerful and frightening emotion.

Anger is a potentially dangerous emotion because of the actual
harm it does, both to the angry person and the recipient of his
anger. Angry feelings are, of themselves, not sinful. However,
anger can lead to distorted perceptions and increased aggression.
If we give in to our anger and hurt someone (either physically or
psychologically) because we are angry, or if we hold on to our
anger for such a long time that we are unable to respond lovingly,
then we may indeed commit a sin. Murderous anger and hatred
are gravely wrong, the Catechism tells us (2302).

WHEN IS ANGER HELPFUL?

Anger can be appropriate to the situation and even praisewor-
thy. When Christ became angry at the Pharisees and called them

"whitewashed tombs" (Matthew 23:27) or when he used a whip on the money changers in the temple (21:12-13), he was responding with righteous anger. Many times God himself is described in the Old Testament as being angry (for example, Numbers 22:22 says, "But now the anger of God flared up"). And in Jesus' parable about the great feast, when the master of the house discovers that everyone is too busy to come to the wedding feast, he becomes enraged and sends out his servant to invite the poor, the crippled, the blind, and the lame (Luke 14:16-24). These are all instances of righteous anger. Anger can impel us to take action against injustice or evil, fight through obstacles to achieve a difficult goal, or express ourselves more passionately and convincingly. Fr. Basil Maturin writes, "Anger is the sword which God puts into man's hand to fight the great moral battles of life."[71]

Like all emotions, anger can be useful because it can be very motivating. For example, when we see an injustice being committed (whether a racial or religious injustice, an obstruction of truth or justice, an abuse of power, or the taking of an innocent life), anger motivates us to work for a change. Sometimes we are angry at ourselves for our own failures and are motivated to change. Anger can also transform fear into action and be used to protect ourselves, our families, or our country. Sometimes we feel anger at the same time as fear—for example, in a threatening situation in which I must fight back to ensure my safety. The expression of anger can also inform other people that the situation is serious. If I speak angrily to my teenage son after he has failed to come home by curfew, this anger will let him know how serious his transgression is.

OUR INDIVIDUAL WAYS OF EXPRESSING ANGER

You've heard the expression "He has a short fuse." Some people, by temperament, tend to become easily angered. Cholerics and sanguines are noted for their quick tempers; sanguines, however, are equally quick to forgive and forget. Cholerics and melancholics tend to hold on to their anger, though the melancholic may turn his anger inward or show it in a more passive-aggressive manner. Even the easygoing phlegmatic at times may have a slow-burning anger that he doesn't think is worth discussing or acting upon. But over time it can build up, and the typically calm temperament can become an out-of-control volcano. Extraverts may express their upset feelings outwardly in angry words and gestures and by blaming others, while introverts may hold them in or take out their feelings on themselves and become sad, fearful, or even depressed.

Our cultural background is also a factor in our emotional responses. Cultures help to "calibrate emotional responding to culturally relevant situations."[72] For example, some cultures are known for their expressivity and volatility, while others are often associated with calm and even dispassionate temperaments.[73] In any case, whether due to temperament or cultural bias, some people do have a short fuse and are easily roused to anger while others are more calm and peaceful. The key is to be aware of these tendencies in advance, to recognize the real source of the anger, and to express anger appropriately.[74]

Inappropriate Expressions
of Anger

There are times, however, when our anger is inappropriate. For example, I might curse at the car that cut me off in traffic, rage at my spouse when I am actually angry at a colleague at work, or throw things in a tantrum. There are other inappropriate ways of showing anger too. Constantly complaining, rolling our eyes, giving the "silent treatment," or ignoring a spouse can be passive-aggressive and inappropriate ways of expressing anger. Anger may reveal a bad habit or immaturity ("I am angry because I didn't get my way"). Excessive anger (screaming at a toddler who spills his milk or nursing vengeful thoughts) or misplaced anger (kicking the dog because I was frustrated at work) is inordinate and inappropriate.

Anger can be a very complex emotion. Sometimes we react angrily to a provocation that isn't really the source of our anger. Sometimes anger masks a deep-seated emotional wound (I become enraged when my boss criticizes me because it triggers feelings of being unloved as a child). Instead of being the sword that fights great moral battles for God, anger can be turned selfishly inward. It can become the weapon that drives loved ones apart and kills the very life of grace in our souls.

If it is possible to take a deep breath, step back from the situation, and take an honest look at ourselves (why are we feeling so angry?), then we might be able to assess our reaction. Am I angry because I didn't get my way? Or is my anger appropriate to the situation? If Art had promised to come home for a family dinner, and he showed up long after the kids were in bed, then

Laraine is justifiably angry. But instead of seething at the sink, angrily crashing the dishes together, she should calmly and lovingly tell him how upset she is that he did not keep his promise. She might say, "I appreciate how hard you work to support us. But I have asked you time and again to come home on time. You promised to do so. I am really angry, and we must talk about this when we both calm down, because this is not right for me, for the kids, or for you." Oftentimes calmly expressing our feelings of anger and disappointment actually diffuses the anger, whereas silently seething fuels it.

We may be a little afraid of our own capacity for anger. Many people try to "stuff" those feelings and sometimes wind up acting out passive-aggressively instead.[75] In marriage counseling, clients sometimes say that the reason they withdraw from conflict or avoid situations and even their loved ones is that they fear an escalation into an ugly and scary scene involving abusive language or worse. Fear of anger or being out of control in such situations causes us to withdraw. But often these "underreactions" lead to overreactions later.

If we have a tendency to underreact or to avoid conflict, we should learn how to express our needs and concerns in a way that does not escalate when problems are addressed. Perhaps we believe that we should "preserve the peace" at all costs—even to the point of denying our own legitimate needs. Perhaps we were raised in a home where it was considered wrong to express feelings. But the better choice is to learn to express our feelings appropriately—rationally, calmly, lovingly, and directly. This is an alternative to "flight or fight." Learning communication skills and constructive alternatives will help us connect positively and share our deepest thoughts and emotions—without angrily escalating.

The renowned marriage researcher John Gottman discovered that all couples (even the happily married ones) will sometimes fight and utter angry words that they later regret. But this is different from a contempt-laden marriage or the pattern of unhappily married couples who use stonewalling or silent withdrawal. Gottman's research shows that it's not so much the occasional fight or expression of anger that can cause trouble in a marriage but a pattern of constant criticism, defensiveness, contempt, and stonewalling.[76] All of these actions harm marriages and relationships, but contempt is the most poisonous of all.

When spouses are treated with contempt, they feel that their marital problems are so severe they cannot be resolved, and they often become ill over the next few years.[77] Simple anger does not have the same reaction. A person who is contemptuous views the other person as inferior, asserts power, and shows disdain and no empathy. Beneath contempt is usually a long-simmering state of habitual anger. Contempt makes loving, respectful, and affectionate communication nearly impossible.

What Can I Do about My Anger?

If you think you have a problem with anger (whether due to a short fuse or a long-simmering resentment), it is wise to know ahead of time what usually triggers your anger. The key question to ask yourself is *"What is the source of my anger?"* Usually it will be a combination of the particular event (my boss was dismissive, my daughter was disrespectful, my friend ignored me) and my own particular vulnerabilities or past wounds. Perhaps I am a bit prideful and suffer mightily when rejected, or I am controlling and fly into a fury when I am ignored, or because of a past wound, I am suspicious and hostile toward authority figures. It may also be that I am simply in an irritable mood and ready to become angry at the least provocation. It's often a combination of the event and my own psychological situation (whether present or past) that affects my tendency to be angry.

Let's imagine that you had a bad day at work, perhaps because your boss rejected your new proposal and you felt frustrated and unappreciated. When you arrive home, you are hungry, tired, and already somewhat irritable. Then, when you ask your daughter whether she has completed her homework and she continues texting her friends before answering you, you blow up in anger and yell at her to have more respect. Typically you don't get angry as soon as you walk in the door. But when you ask yourself, "*What is the source of my anger?*" you realize that it was the fact that you had not directly addressed the problem at work. You were feeling rejected, disappointed, and frustrated, and these feelings were the real source of your anger—not so much your daughter's behavior. Sure, she was irritating, but typically you would not have blown your top. Tonight, however, already feeling upset and frustrated, you were like a simmering pot ready to explode. That is why it is so important to know ourselves and to monitor our feelings and address them when they are manageable rather than waiting until we explode or our feelings are already out of control.

If you know ahead of time that you are easily roused to anger when you have had a bad day at work, when you are running late, or when someone disagrees with you, flouts your authority, or ignores you, then you can prepare for such situations with a healthier and more Christian response. You can take a deep breath, say a prayer for strength and wisdom, count to ten, and use empathy to try to put yourself in the other person's shoes. When you tell yourself, "He didn't mean it the way it sounds" or "I've always had a history of feeling rejected when someone criticizes me" or "He's been out of work for six months, so he is having a hard time," you will be better able to maintain self-control and emotional regulation.

Handling our anger maturely doesn't mean we have to bottle up our feelings. As St. Paul wrote to the Ephesians, "Be angry but do not sin" (4:26). We can deal with the situation appropriately. Handling the situation maturely means that we express ourselves calmly and rationally, stick to the topic that made us angry, and speak with the appropriate person. We do not, for example, take out our anger on the children by yelling at them or on our spouse by bringing up unrelated mistakes that he or she made two years ago.

WHEN IS ANGER SINFUL?

Jesus highlights the dangers of anger, particularly in the Gospel of Matthew. His words seem very severe; he proposes it as an extension of the Mosaic commandment "You shall not kill" (Exodus 20:13). Christ, who fulfills the law, looks beyond our external keeping of the commandments and into the depths of our hearts. If emotions are not sinful in themselves, why does he tell us that our anger might condemn us? "But I say to you, whoever is angry with his brother will be liable to judgment . . .

, and whoever says, 'You fool,' will be liable to fiery Gehenna" (Matthew 5:22). Jesus then immediately admonishes us to be reconciled with our brother before coming to the altar (5:23-24).

We may well wonder whether Jesus can actually mean that calling someone a fool is risking damnation! Scripture scholars have speculated that what Christ is condemning here is the *habit* of being angry rather than a one-time emotion.[78] Being in a chronic state of anger is poisonous to the soul.

It is a psychological and spiritual truth that anger is divisive. We have all had the experience of thinking about someone or something that has offended us in the past and becoming angry all over again. Sometimes we even dwell on the apparent misdeed or insult. We find ourselves growing angry, resentful, and possibly even vengeful. Though our initial moment of anger was not in itself sinful (it was not intentional or willed), deliberately dwelling on the thoughts that give rise to our anger may indeed be sinful.

That is why anger is called one of the seven deadly sins. As an emotion, anger is not in itself sinful; however, it can certainly lead to sin. Fr. Emmerich Vogt explains that anger is not sinful if the cause of the anger is just, if the anger is no greater than the cause demands, and if we let go of the anger after we have taken appropriate action. Anger as a "deadly sin" is actually unjust anger, anger that is "excessive, revengeful, and out of control."[79] The Catechism tells us that vengeful anger (seeking revenge as opposed to justice for wrongdoing) and deliberate hatred are sins against the fifth commandment. Hatred is deliberately wishing our neighbor evil. If we deliberately wish that someone encounter grave harm, then our sin is also grave (CCC, 2303).

Being perpetually angry or resentful (or being vengeful) is different from an outburst of anger. Feelings of ongoing resentment and anger are often caused by a sense of shame, perhaps as a result of trauma (see chapter 8). Sometimes we try to avoid feelings of discouragement, rejection, disempowerment, or worthlessness by masking them with anger. If I have low self-esteem and someone makes a critical comment, I might respond in anger to mask my feelings of unworthiness. Responding angrily gives me a temporary and false feeling of being in control by putting someone else down, and it temporarily relieves my anxiety or sense of shame. Of course, soon thereafter the self-loathing and feelings of powerlessness and shame return.[80]

A constant state of anger that seeks to belittle people ultimately separates us from our colleagues, friends, and loved ones. Lasting anger gives rise to hatred, resentment, contempt, and thoughts of revenge. It is this deliberate, lasting anger that is sinful. We do not love when we persist in our anger. We also may become unjust, for when our anger is unforgiving or seeks revenge, we are behaving like the wicked servant who, after having been shown mercy, refuses to show mercy to his fellow servant who owed him less than he had owed the master (Matthew 18:21-35).

Habitual Anger, Resentment, or Abuse

Psychologist Steven Stosny, author and founder of Compassion Power[81] in the Washington, D.C. metropolitan area, has treated more than six thousand clients for problems related to anger, abuse, and violence. His innovative anger-management workshops and training are successful in reducing and even eliminating resentment, contempt, and abuse in the lives of angry people. Dr. Stosny has discovered that underlying all resentment (and anger and abuse) is a core hurt—guilt, shame, and anxiety about our self-worth. Compassion (both for yourself and for others) is the key to getting rid of hidden resentment and ultimately preventing anger problems.[82]

If you live with someone who has a serious and habitual anger problem, then you will often find yourself having to carefully tiptoe around the minefield of that person's simmering anger, bad moods, derogatory statements, angry blowups, criticism, and negative judgments. You refrain from saying what you think to avoid triggering a blowup. You become hypersensitive to your spouse's moods. You tell the kids, "Be quiet. Daddy's in a bad mood." You start wondering whether you *ought* to say what you feel or think. Your own self-confidence may begin to disappear. Worse, you may submit to your angry partner's emotional or even physical abuse. This is wrong. The angry spouse or relative must receive therapy, and the spouse who is abused must stop being a victim. Says Stosny, "Your compassionate demand for change is likely to be the only thing that will motivate him [the angry spouse] to once again be the man you married."[83]

Stosny describes the adrenalin rush that occurs when we become enraged as a "drug" that angry, contemptuous people need in order to reduce the pain in their lives. It also provides temporary feelings of superiority and self-righteousness as they hammer away at someone. But these feelings do not last. And, as we noted before, after a rampage, they are left with guilt, remorse, depression, and a feeling of being disconnected from those they love.

COMPASSION COUNTERACTS ANGER

Can we change such behavior? First, any sort of abusive behavior must stop. This might require therapy or a call to 911, but the angry person has to stop acting out. Then, once everyone is calm, the resentment, shame, self-loathing, and distorted beliefs can be addressed. Stosny believes that compassion, which is a 180-degree turn from resentment or chronic anger, is the solution. The tide of resentment and chronic anger turns around when the person struggling with anger actively shows others how much he values and loves them through overtly compassionate acts. In addition, the angry person needs to be compassionate toward himself by trying to recognize the core hurts that he is managing by being angry or resentful.

Stosny highlights four key features of compassion, each of which chips away at resentment, anger, and contempt: (1) protecting other people, (2) affirming other people, (3) connecting with others, and (4) initiating good things for others. Stosny recommends that his angry clients consciously remind themselves of these four attitudes and actively integrate them into their lives. Let's consider an example of compassion in action.

Sean is a hardworking husband and father who has a stressful and dangerous job as a police officer. He is often exhausted when he returns home, and he just wants to relax. But his habitual bad mood upon returning home often erupts into anger at the slightest provocation. Everyone tries to stay out of his way, and the kids are afraid to ask him for help with their schoolwork.

To counteract his tendency toward anger, Sean practices the four aspects of compassion. Knowing that he is most vulnerable to angry outbursts when he returns from work, he develops a new routine. Before he enters the house, he sits in his car in the driveway and takes a moment to say a prayer of thanksgiving, asking God for the strength to be patient and loving with his family. He waits until he is calm and peaceful. Then, he enters the home ready to protect, affirm, connect, and initiate the good.[84]

First, he protects. He checks on the teens to make sure they are safe as they chat with their friends on the Internet. He removes the shoes from the front of the doorway so that nobody will trip on them. He actively protects his family.

Second, Sean affirms each family member. He asks the kids about their day and gives them hugs. He gives his wife a kiss and asks how her day was, even if he doesn't feel like listening to her answer. He listens without interrupting.

Third, he connects. He wants to have a beer and watch some TV by himself, but he stays in the kitchen, listening to his wife. He offers to help in setting the table for dinner. He chats with each family member. If he owes anyone an apology, he takes the first step to make amends and heal the relationship.

Finally, he initiates good things. Sean calls everyone to dinner and leads the family in prayer. He asks each family member to talk about what happened that day or to express a concern. He listens and offers help if needed. He discusses upcoming events such as vacations or concerts that are good for the family. By protecting, affirming, initiating the good, and connecting with others, Sean becomes a more compassionate husband and father, and he transforms his angry or resentful feelings into feelings of love, peace, and joy.

Some of us may have such hair-trigger reactions or deep-seated wounds that it would be exceedingly difficult to follow the four steps of compassion described here. In some cases, a past wound needs to be healed in order to allow the transformational power of compassion to enter in. If so, we may need professional help so that our anger does not become harmful to ourselves or others.

Though Dr. Stosny is a secular psychologist, his emphasis on compassion, a Christian virtue, is one that we Catholics are called to practice. The parable of the Good Samaritan highlights compassion in action. Jesus tells us that the Samaritan was "moved with compassion at the sight" of the man beaten by robbers and left for dead on the side of the road. Who was the neighbor to the victim? "The one who treated him with mercy." Jesus tells us: "Go and do likewise" (Luke 10:33, 37). Thus, compassion *is* mercy. And we are commanded to treat others with mercy if we hope to be treated mercifully ourselves. "Be merciful, just as your Father is merciful" (Luke 6:36). This is what it means to love our enemies. St. Paul tells us: "Love is patient, love is kind. It is not jealous, is not pompous, it is not inflated, . . . it is not quick-tempered, it does not brood over injury" (1 Corinthians 13:4-5). Love and compassion transform us and enrich our lives and relationships. With the grace of God, love can turn back resentment and contempt.

We have all experienced contempt, and we may have been contemptuous ourselves, but Christ can transform our hearts. With God's grace and with the help of the sacraments, we can find the strength to triumph over anger and contempt in our lives. As we strive to grow in the virtues of humility, patience, and meekness, we can recite this short prayer: "Jesus, meek and humble of heart, make my heart like unto thine." We can begin to forgive others and show them mercy, slowly chipping away at any long-standing resentment. Transforming contempt and anger into love and respect is an inside-out change, from our hearts and souls to our behavior and interactions.

Going Further

1. Proverbs 14:17 says, "The quick-tempered man makes a fool of himself, / but the prudent man is at peace." Scripture is not necessarily impugning one's natural tendency (usually by temperament) to be quick-tempered. If we, by nature, have a rather short fuse, this is not a sin. However, God does not want us to justify our sinful behavior by saying, "I can't help it; that's just the way I am." We notice that the quick-tempered man is juxtaposed with the prudent man. Scripture posits the ideal of *prudently* assessing our responses (just as we have suggested in this book). Is it wise to erupt in anger over that small transgression? If not, then we should not act on that angry feeling. That would be foolish! Can you think of instances in your own life in which you, perhaps imprudently, acted on an impulsive response? Do you think it might have been possible to cool down and then act more prudently? What are some steps you can take to respond more prudently in the future?

2. Love "is quick-tempered, it does not brood over injury" (1 Corinthians 13:5). This is tough, especially for married couples! Sometimes we behave better (more patiently, more judiciously

with our language) with our co-workers or acquaintances than with our loved ones. We may say harsh words that we later regret, or we may yell at our kids. In such cases, it is always necessary to ask for forgiveness. As St. Paul says, "Do not let the sun set on your anger" (Ephesians 4:26). Can you name some of the ways you might be showing resentment or harboring anger toward your loved ones?

If you are married, do you find yourself counting up your spouse's transgressions or holding grudges? Do you hold on to a particular failure and return to it again and again in your mind? Do you find yourself responding by rolling your eyes, making snippy or sarcastic comments, or muttering under your breath? Or do you hide behind a closed door, or in front of a computer or TV screen, or in overactivity with your kids? There are many ways to distance yourself from your spouse and avoid intimacy. If resentment and contempt is threatening your marriage, it would be wise to seek professional help.

3. Do you know what triggers your anger? Are there any steps you can take to avoid or prepare in advance for these triggers? For example, if you find that you are especially irritable and prone to angry outbursts when you are tired and hungry, then make sure you have a good night's sleep and are well nourished before you undertake that challenging project with the annoying co-worker. When you feel yourself growing angry, plan in advance the calming steps you can take. For example, you might try to take a deep breath, count to ten, remove yourself from the situation, say a Hail Mary or a prayer to the Holy Spirit, or try to put yourself in the other person's shoes.

Can you think of other steps you can take to foster a sense of peace in the midst of a stressful or angry situation?

4. St. Francis de Sales suggested practicing meekness, kindness, and benevolence during those times when we are not feeling the heat of anger, thereby practicing these virtues in advance of the time when we will really need them. Look over the past few days. How often did you practice these virtues? How can you change your routine or behavior so that these virtues become a more regular part of your life?

CHAPTER 8

PAST WOUNDS AND PRESENT TRIALS

*Suffering, personal imperfection, and emotional problems
have never been satisfactorily explained, yet many saints have
found in their faith in the Living Christ the means to fill
every void with Presence and love.*[85]
—Brother Lawrence of the Resurrection

Juan was a single accomplished professional in his midforties when he came to counseling because of feelings of loneliness and depression.[86] Juan's emotional state was causing him to be distracted and to underperform at work, and recently he had been overreacting to minor setbacks on the job.

Juan struggled not only with depression but also with a lack of close relationships. He tended to feel insecure in personal relationships and feared being rejected. As a result, he mistrusted people and doubted whether he had anything to contribute or whether people would really like and love him.

When asked about his childhood, Juan described it generally as a blank with few memories worth noting. He described more involvement with his mother, but he often expressed resentment about her intrusiveness into his private affairs. Of late they were not on good terms because they argued so frequently about almost everything.

Juan's father was never physically abusive, but he was emotionally absent from Juan's life. Although he was around throughout Juan's childhood and his parents stayed married, Juan had very few memories of doing anything with his father. Juan excelled in school, but even with his excellent grades, he could not remember a compliment from his father. He described his dad as a distant, detached, uninterested workaholic with whom he had never felt connected or close. Art asked Juan if he felt that he was special in his dad's eyes, and Juan replied, "Not at all. I got the impression that he was generally disappointed in me."

Juan was reluctant to talk about his relationship with his father. "It was mostly my fault," said Juan. "How was that?" Art asked. "Well, when I was about twelve years old, my dad asked me to throw a football with him. I wasn't able to catch his spirals, and I kept throwing uncatchable wobbly throws back to him. My dad said if I couldn't do any better than that, he wasn't going to play catch with me. Then he shook his head and went back into the house." Juan was noticeably sad when telling this story. Art asked, "What happened next?" "Nothing," Juan replied. "That was the last time we ever played football."

Curiously, Juan saw his dad's refusal to play catch again as his own fault and not his dad's. Juan felt that because he was so lousy at throwing a football, he had disappointed his father and that his own inadequacy hurt their relationship. Juan was far from being the beloved son of his father.[87]

It is not the child's responsibility to engender a relationship with the parents; it's the parents' responsibility to care for their child and establish a warm and loving relationship. But Juan didn't think or feel that way. He felt helpless to fix the problem and deep shame that he had let his father down. This is how children tend to think about these issues, and it is also how many adults think about past traumas and rejection when they reflect on their childhood experiences. The childhood understanding becomes the false reality of how they see themselves, even into adulthood.

Juan's shame that his father's rejection of him was his own fault, as well as his feelings of helplessness, reveal the traumatic nature of the event in Juan's life—one that affected his emotional balance and caused sexual-attraction issues in his adult life. Juan's emotional wound has had a serious impact on his ability to regulate his emotions and to have healthy and intimate relationships.

We all suffer the consequences of original sin that cause us to struggle with integration and living a healthy life. In addition, some of us have traumatic wounds that have a more severe impact on our sense of identity and self-worth, on our relations with others, and often on our relationship with God.

In this chapter we are going to talk about how the wounds of untreated and unhealed traumatic incidents can wreak havoc with our emotions and thereby cause difficulties in our personal and interpersonal lives. We will look at how past wounds affect our ability to trust, to regulate our emotions, to be intimate, and to find happiness. We will also discuss what we can do to achieve healing and to help those who have experienced a traumatic incident. These wounds contribute to unhealthy emotional reactions and impulsive or imprudent responses that can alienate us from others, leaving us angry, bitter, and alone. But healing these emotional wounds is possible. This healing is often a matter of integrating the psychological and spiritual aspects of ourselves, and can involve the family in the process.

TRAUMATIC WOUNDS, OUR EMOTIONS, AND OUR RELATIONSHIPS

"Trauma" is a Greek word meaning "wound" or "injury." The Latin word *injuria* means "to wrong." Trauma not only injures but can leave the injured person feeling helpless and unable to cope—especially if the injured person did not receive adequate support and recovery from loved ones. Physician Meg Meeker offers the example of a young girl who was raped on a date. This was a horrible experience for her. But just as traumatic was the lack of response from her father, who said, "Boys will be boys" as he headed out to play golf. His complete abandonment of his daughter after this traumatic event left her feeling helpless and ashamed.[88] Meeker points out that the father's nonresponsiveness was as responsible for the girl's trauma as the event itself.

In the words of one psychologist, this "helplessness is the essence of trauma."[89] Trauma often leaves us with a feeling of shame and a mistrust of others and the world. The traumatized person thinks: *"Since I was abused or mistreated, there must be something wrong with me."* This "double hit" (the world is unsafe; I am fundamentally unworthy) is the scar that leads to further emotional and relationship wounds. It sets up an insecure foundation that hinders the development of a healthy emotional life.[90]

Maureen Canning, an expert on sex addictions at The Meadows in Arizona, describes the shame that sexually abused victims feel, but it is common to many other traumatic events as well:

When a child's instinctual needs for love, physical care, and coaching go unmet, the memory of that deprivation becomes imprinted in his psyche. Because the child believes it is because of his own inadequacy that his needs are not being fulfilled, his personality and his life come to be shame-based. All trauma gets its power from this original shaming.[91]

For many, the traumatic event was specific (such as molestation, beatings, witnessing something horrific), but for others, like Juan, it can be an ongoing sense of neglect or absence of affection from a key person like a parent. Unmet emotional needs can result in fears of abandonment and rejection (which, in turn, can give rise to anxious, depressed, or angry feelings) and in shame (causing feelings of rage and guilt).[92]

COMPENSATING FOR A SENSE OF SHAME

A victim can spend his or her life trying to avoid triggering the helpless and shameful feelings that arise unbidden. Feelings of helplessness and self-loathing take a tremendous toll on personal integrity and interpersonal relationships. Yet we can be unaware of this toll. We remember, perhaps, the harm others did to us, but it is hard to see—and often it is the pain of seeing it that makes it so difficult—how our own woundedness affects our present and future relationships. We may overreact or underreact emotionally, become oversensitive or overly critical, or use alcohol or other substances in an (often unconscious) attempt to alleviate the pain from the emotional wound.

Some who have suffered neglect or abuse might try to overcome the sense of shame and helplessness by dominating or controlling others—screaming at family members, for example, or being overly critical or contemptuous. They might have a sense that "nobody responds to my requests," just as their cries for help as a child went unanswered. Or they might isolate themselves and discount any opportunity to trust and be intimate. An adult beaten as a child might try to manage that sense of being victimized by in turn victimizing others, perhaps his own children. Some people with insecure attachments from childhood might become anxious, clingy, and emotionally needy as adults.[93] Some "self-medicate" to deaden the wound by sexual addictions or by overeating or drinking. Addictions and compulsions can be ritualized attempts to primitively manage and try to repair traumatic wounds by acting out or medicating the pain that we don't know how to address or the uncontrollable emotions that we fear might erupt.

If we repeatedly respond in an emotionally inappropriate way, it may indicate that we have a wound related to rejection or a more serious trauma. Like Juan's overreacting to criticism or Monica's flying into a rage, our reaction shows that we have some personal issues that need to be addressed. In other words, it says more about *us* than it does about the other person. As we become emotionally and spiritually healthy, we have the support and ability not only to look "out there" when something goes wrong but also to look inside ourselves. Then we can ask ourselves, "What wound just received a blow that hurts so much?" God allows such situations so that we can have the opportunity to grow in self-awareness and to eventually detach from our insecurities and begin to heal our wounds.

Traumatic wounds affect our emotions in three key areas:

1. My self-concept. Who am I? Instead of seeing myself as a person with dignity made in God's image and likeness, as being a beloved child of God, I may see myself from a more shame-based perspective: There is something wrong with me, and I am somehow to blame. This self-loathing can eclipse happiness and self-confidence, which are so necessary for a healthy emotional and personal life.

2. My relationships. It can be difficult to respond in a healthy way in intimate relationships with traumatic wounds. If my emotional foundation is insecure, I am often distrustful of others and may fear intimacy. I may respond automatically with either "fight" or "flight." But these two options do not foster close connections with others. I may fear further betrayal—that others will see how awful I am or that they will hurt me or take advantage of me. So I keep others at a distance, or I control my surroundings in an unhealthy way, or I make everyone walk on eggshells lest I explode. If the trauma was caused by a caregiver or a close family member (sometimes called "attachment figures"), future close relationships may be seen not as a source of security but as a source of danger.

3. My relationship with God. Often there is anger toward God for allowing this traumatic event and its repercussions to happen. Such anger is, of itself, not sinful. But anger can lead me to reject or mistrust God and thereby miss out on his healing power. Or my concept of God may be that he is cold,

uncaring, distant, or cruel. This distortion leaves me isolated and vulnerable.

FIGHT OR FLIGHT

Because the interpersonal dynamics of trauma tend to generalize to other similar intimate or trusting situations, trauma's harmful effects can expand. The feelings of helplessness, shame, and pain can cause us to feel afraid in almost any interpersonal situation, particularly one with conflict. Fr. Emmerich Vogt often highlights the fact that *fear is the primary activator of our faults.* This may be why Jesus told us so many times to *be not afraid*, for fear can eclipse or diminish love. "There is no fear in love, but perfect love drives out fear" (1 John 4:18). It is love that saves, empowers, and transforms us. Fear (and other insecurities) can restrict our reactions to two options: fight or flight. There are times when each response is prudent. If I am in danger, flight may be appropriate. If I am facing an injustice, fighting may be justified. Jesus did the same with the money changers in the temple (Matthew 21:12-13).

However, traumatic wounds sometimes cause us to react in fight-or-flight mode when it is imprudent or ill-advised. For example, if I am at work and my boss points out some errors in my work, it would be imprudent to become combative and demand to see the HR director. It would also be irrational to burst into tears at the criticism or leave the office. Yet if the criticism triggered my insecurities because of a past emotional wound, I may be reacting out of fear.

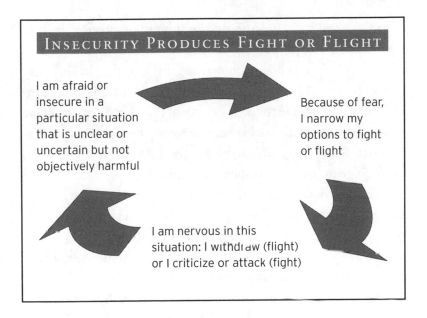

THE WOUND EXPOSED

Often you hear people say, "Just get over it! Whatever it was, it happened a long time ago, so you just need to stop crying about it!" Of course, the traumatized person would love to "get over it." But if you have a knee injury that forces you to limp, you probably will not find it helpful if someone tells you, "*Pick it up and run faster, slowpoke. Get over it!*" You need to see a doctor and get the knee repaired. Emotionally traumatic wounds are similar. We need to treat them so that we can become healthy. Pretending we are healed, denying the issue, or trying to avoid the problem doesn't help. And in prayer we may find God encouraging us to address the issues, to get help, and to heal. Repair work is needed here.

Let's return to Juan. At work he submitted a rough draft of a new marketing proposal to his boss to be sure that he was on the right track. His boss, somewhat gruff at times, liked Juan's proposal overall, but he did make a few comments that were critical. Juan was unable to focus on any of the positive areas; all he heard were the criticisms. He became simultaneously enraged that his boss was so impossible to please and ashamed that he was so inadequate in his job and such a failure.

Juan returned home depressed and despondent. At work the next day, he shut his office door and brooded. He did not return phone calls and did not speak to anyone all day. He also was unable to focus on his work, so he spent his time surfing the Web because he felt he was unappreciated at work anyway.

Juan's wound was exposed, his boss had brushed up against it, and Juan was reeling in pain. His boss's criticisms triggered the memories of his dad's dissatisfaction and his own shame. Juan sees criticism as an attack on his character, his abilities, his competence, and even his self-worth. He was both angry and despairing.

Later, when Juan was calm, he realized that the criticisms were not personal attacks nor were they serious criticisms of his work. There were only a few corrections he needed to make. Yet this incident made him realize that he was, perhaps, jeopardizing his job by his emotional overreactions whenever he faced everyday bumps in the road. He needed to deal with the past wound that was causing him to have unhealthy emotional reactions.

The problem of living solely and exclusively on the level of fight or flight is that emotional engagement and commitment are nearly impossible. Imagine if you feel that any conflict will leave you either arguing and fighting or feeling alone or abandoned. Then it is hard to commit and connect.

Acknowledging the Wound

Juan is beginning to realize that the problems are not just "out there," but inside himself. So he has started to get some two-pronged help. He has made a commitment to his spiritual growth and is able to meet monthly for spiritual direction with his pastor. At the same time, he has started seeing a Catholic clinician. In therapy Juan has learned that his emotional wounds sometimes prevent him from reacting calmly, prudently, and appropriately.

For Juan, the first step toward healing is to *become aware* of his tendency to react inappropriately when faced with an emotional trigger. This first step, awareness, helps Juan grow in self-knowledge, self-acceptance, and humility. Juan has discovered that his overreactions are not due primarily to present circumstances but indicate the presence of an internal, unresolved wound. With the help of his therapist, Juan has learned to look for options other than fight or flight. He reminds himself: "Even though I asked my boss for his feedback and I am well aware that he may have to make some necessary criticisms, I also know myself well enough to know that I am vulnerable to criticism. I know why that is: It's my old father wound. I need to prepare myself for feeling disappointed, and remind myself that he is not rejecting me, nor am I a complete failure. It's painful but not devastating."

Now, after meeting with his boss, Juan says a quick prayer, pulls out a yellow legal pad, and makes a list of his boss's comments on his proposal, both good and bad. He tries to keep both sets of comments at a distance by detaching himself from their impact. He also challenges the "automatic thoughts" that put him in the fight-or-flight defensive posture: "My boss is not saying I am horrible when he offers constructive criticism on my proposal. He is helping me improve my work and is not making judgments on my character." Juan finds that he is beginning to think more clearly and rationally, which affects how he feels in a positive way. He can even admit that many of the comments his boss has made were very helpful. He realizes that he can remain confident in his work even though his pride may have taken a few blows.

After a counseling session, Juan makes the suggested changes and brings them to his boss. Juan has to fight his tendency to just drop off the changes and leave without talking to his boss. He thanks his boss for the constructive criticism, and his boss tells him that he appreciates Juan's cooperation. Juan has discovered that when he discusses these things—as opposed to avoiding them—he feels better. He even tells his boss about several areas in which he disagreed with him. In the past this was very difficult for Juan to do without storming about defensively or sulking in his office. Yet now he has learned something new: If he responds honestly and openly, his boss respects him more. Juan has discovered that his relationships are strengthened when he is honest and open and when he regulates the expression of his emotion instead of avoiding or escalating.

JESUS' HEALING PRESENCE

Juan does not wrestle with this issue alone. He knows that Jesus loves him and died for him (John 3:16), that he gives rest to all who are weary (Matthew 11:28), and that his promise to us is peace (John 14:27) and an abundant life (10:10). These words and the person of Christ he has met though the sacraments, in prayer, and in spiritual direction give him the strength and hope to face his wound. Jesus is no longer a distant stranger to Juan. Through daily prayer, Scripture reading, Mass, and frequent confession, Juan has developed a personal relationship with Christ and now calls on him, his great friend (John 15:15), to be with him when he faces his weakest moments: the wound from his father. Jesus doesn't allow him to run away in fear or anger ("Who needs this place. I'm going to quit and work for someone more appreciative!"). This is not Christian detachment but unhealthy amputation. Instead, Juan knows that Jesus wants him to face his weakness, which is his cross, but he also knows that Jesus will be at his side: "And behold, I am with you always" (Matthew 28:20).

STEPS TO HEALING

Once you become aware that you have a pattern of inappropriate emotional responses, the next step is to realize that the issue is probably not just "out there" (the spouse, the boss, the kids, the weather, the economy, and so forth) but inside of you. This is a very difficult step to take, and sometimes it is filled with shame and self-loathing. These feelings are usually the products of the original trauma, which have left you feeling unworthy, powerless, abandoned, or neglected.

The next step is to get help. Our pride ("I can do it myself"), our vanity ("I don't want to let people know how hurt I am"), or our laziness ("I do not have the time, energy, or money to get help") may prevent us from addressing the issue. There is also the issue of trust. This is often the most difficult barrier: I trusted before, and my trust was abused. How can I trust anyone again?

Traumatic wounds are serious and generally need both spiritual guidance from a qualified priest, deacon, sister, or lay spiritual director and professional help from a qualified therapist. The integration of a spiritual and psychological healing is the best way to address these serious wounds. Often couples counseling can be an important adjunct to individual therapy to help spouses realize when the traumatic wounds might be causing marriage difficulties and how best to respond to them. In fact, a strong marital relationship may help in transforming feelings of abandonment, guilt, or shame to positive feelings of attachment and self-worth. Here are some critical steps in the process of healing that can be addressed with the help of a professional counselor and spiritual director:

1. Create a "safe haven" and a "safe base" in your relationship. The trauma wound can put everyone on edge and in a defensive posture, resulting in more frequent conflict and temptations to alienate (flight) or escalate (fight). By strengthening the healthy emotional attachments (with one's spouse and with a trusted counselor or spiritual director, for example), you can address problems with love and compassion. This step usually requires professional help and education about trauma. Trauma expert Susan Johnson explains that secure, healthy attachments form a "safe haven." We all need healthy emotional attachments, but often these attachments have been

broken for those who have suffered from trauma or abuse, and the victim feels alone and abandoned and fearful about dealing with the trauma. Spouses and family members can help create a supportive and secure environment that is at once both protective and encouraging.[94]

2. Regulate emotions. As we discussed throughout this book, emotional regulation does not mean repressing or eliminating feelings, nor does it mean we should let our emotions run wild. We do, however, need to be aware of the appropriateness of our emotional responses. We can identify emotional triggers to avoid ugly escalations and painful sequences. Once the emotional patterns are identified, we can learn to redirect or respond differently. This rerouting of responses takes time, but it can be done—sometimes with the help of prescribed medication—within a loving and caring environment. Patience, perseverance, and practicing new responses will help along the healing process.

3. Counter dysfunctional or errant automatic thoughts by replacing them with healthier, more realistic thinking, which in turn produces more functional and less exaggerated emotions. Breaking the tyranny of faulty core beliefs frees us to respond in more meaningful and productive ways—for example, facing trials with a peacefulness of soul, rejoicing in another's success, loving what deserves to be loved, and desiring the true good.

4. Collaboratively solve problems. I become more capable of asking others for help. This helps me trust others and

overcome a sense of isolation or of having to solve all problems on my own.

5. Trust self-disclosure and accept such disclosures from others, even if we disagree. I am not disclosing my feelings or thoughts in order to manipulate a response, but I am appropriately sharing my thoughts or feelings because I am a person of dignity, and what I think and feel is important. This is not emotional or cognitive bullying; it is expressing how I think and feel, and then letting the chips fall where they may.

6. Respond with empathy. When trust and self-regulation increase, I am capable of putting myself in the other person's shoes. If I am psychologically vulnerable or unhealthy, I will be limited to a fight-or-flight response when others express strong feelings, especially if I feel criticized. But when I am psychologically and spiritually healthy, I can recognize that others have issues, problems, fears, and concerns. I can return a loving response to another person's anger or criticism.

7. Finally, broaden not only our reactions but also our sense of who we really are. Integrating more psychological and spiritually healthy responses into our sense of self and our relationships (with others and with God) helps us to heal and overcome our traumatic wounds.

Pope Benedict XVI writes about how our woundedness can be an opportunity to invite Christ the Healer into our lives. He acknowledges that suffering is always hard to understand and bear, and even harder to *welcome* as part of our vocation.[95] But he cautions that Christ's ways are not our ways:

> Christ is not a healer in the manner of the world. In order to heal us, he does not remain outside the suffering that is experienced; he eases it by coming to dwell within the one stricken by illness, to bear it and live it with him. Christ doesn't always heal suffering by taking it away, but rather by living it with those who suffer, and bringing them toward the hope of a new creation.[96]

We are no longer alone or isolated in our suffering; Christ is with us. With his help, our suffering can be transformed into a "new creation" (2 Corinthians 5:17). As St. Paul wrote to the Colossians, "Now I rejoice in my sufferings for your sake, and in my flesh I am filling up what is lacking in the afflictions of Christ on behalf of his body, which is the church" (Colossians 1:24).

GOING FURTHER

1. Do you have any "baggage" from your past that slows you down, impairs your ability to be happy, affects your emotional responses, or hinders your relationships? Examine your own emotional reactions, using the following questions:

   • Do I often mistrust my own feelings or the feelings expressed by others?

- Do I fear that my feelings are scary? Have I learned to ignore them?
- Do I have a hard time being aware of my own feelings or acknowledging them?
- Do I tell myself: "It doesn't really matter how *I* feel. I am much more aware of how *you* feel."

2. When you respond inappropriately to a situation or a person, do you tend to blame the other person or situation? What might prevent you from looking deeper within yourself to determine if the event opened up an emotional wound?

3. How would you answer the question "Who am I?" Would you be likely to say that you are a beloved child of God? Or would you be more likely to describe yourself in negative terms? How could Jesus' presence in your life heal you of a negative self-image?

4. Explore the feelings that really trouble you. (Remember that your feelings are not sinful in themselves.) What are some other ways of appropriately expressing your feelings—especially anger about a family member who failed to protect you when you were small or who hurt or abandoned you? If you have very strong, upsetting emotions or past trauma, it may be helpful to share these in a safe and supportive setting, such as with a professional therapist or spiritual director.

5. Boundaries enable us to retain our experience of inner worth amidst outside pressures. They protect our dignity and do not

allow others to make inappropriate demands on us. Boundaries can protect us from unnecessary emotional pain and allow us to appreciate the inherent dignity of others, even when they are acting inappropriately. If we are often feeling angry, resentful, or overwhelmed by life, it may be due to a lack of appropriate boundaries. We may be overcommitted to our work or to our volunteering or overly "enmeshed" with our families. Then we feel that we cannot say no out of fear of rejection or an overly developed desire to please others. Are you able to set appropriate boundaries in your life? If not, how can you do so?

CHAPTER 9

EMOTIONS AND THE SPIRITUAL LIFE

Lord, make me an instrument of your peace;
where there is hatred, let me sow love;
where there is injury, pardon;
where there is doubt, faith;
where there is despair, hope;
where there is darkness, light;
and where there is sadness, joy.
—Prayer of St. Francis

We all struggle with managing and regulating our emotions and passions and keeping a healthy, well-balanced perspective. It's the human condition, thanks to original sin. We were created in the image and likeness of God, and before the Fall, our first parents, Adam and Eve, were completely balanced in their emotional lives. They never became inordinately angry, lustful, or envious.[97] Their relationship with God, with each other, with themselves, and even with the world was harmonious. Their lives were perfectly ordered.

Then Adam and Eve sinned. The harmonious relationships were broken. Because of original sin, which has been passed on to all their descendents, we sometimes doubt God's love, we sometimes treat each other badly, and we may suffer from mood swings, anxiety, debilitating fear, and out-of-control anger. We can behave irrationally and are prone to sin. Even good and noble emotions such as love and desire can turn into lust, envy, and greed. Theologian Fr. Adolphe Tanquerey, author of the classic *The Spiritual Life*, lists four effects of disordered passions:[98]

1. *Our soul is blinded.* Our minds become clouded by emotion, and we are less capable of seeing clearly the will of God and more prone to indulging in the feelings of the moment.

2. *We become wearied—and even tortured—by our mood changes and insistent desires.* St. John of the Cross says that the passions are like "impatient little children that can never be pleased, that ask their mother now for this, now for that, and are never satisfied."[99] (Consider the man who drinks excessively, and then, to assuage his feelings of anxiety and guilt, returns to the very habit that tortured his soul.) Only God, who is infinite, can satisfy our desires. As St. Augustine famously wrote, "Our hearts are restless, O Lord, until they rest in you."

3. *Our will becomes weak.* Every concession we make to an ill-ordered passion (a desire for something—even something good—without considering the will of God) weakens our will, and we become ever more lax and lukewarm. Our energy to do the right thing and to follow Christ decreases.

4. *We lose our focus.* We lose that awareness of our calling to higher and better things. We become more focused on the things of the world or the pleasures of the senses than to God.

And these attachments cause us to be anxious and fearful of losing them. Jesus came to free us from these attachments so that we can be free from having to respond in fear, so that we can respond with love. We become what we love. If we are drawn to the lower things of life, then we cannot become what we are called to be—to the high and noble calling to become like Christ. As St. Paul wrote to the Philippians, "Our citizenship is in heaven" (3:20).

GOD'S HEALING PLAN

God is love, and he wants us to experience his joy. Every human being is drawn to and loves what is good. We don't love evil. Rather, we fear, hate, are saddened by, or become angry in the face of evil (CCC, 1765). Scripture repeatedly tells us (some say 365 times!) to fear not. Fear is opposed to love, but "perfect love drives out fear" (1 John 4:18). Not only does perfect love (God himself) free us from fear, but our efforts to love more perfectly (that is, to love with Christ's love) can dispel our own fears.

What makes us fearful? Perhaps, deep down, beneath the scars of past and present wounds, we fear abandonment, isolation, and worthlessness. Pope Benedict XVI says that the ultimate fear that every human being faces is complete aloneness and existential abandonment. "In the last analysis all the fear in the world is the fear of this loneliness . . . the loneliness into which love can no longer advance."[100]

To keep this fear at bay, we turn to many other things. We cling to our possessions, our status, or our ways of coping. We have to be right or perfect or in control. But these attachments or ways of coping are limited. When someone challenges us or we are in danger of losing these things, we become afraid, anxious, or angry. We may become guarded, overly cautious, critical, mistrustful of others, and afraid to take chances and to grow. We lose our sense of peace and balance, and our lives become narrow, miserly, and less loving.

This is not the way God intended for us to live, and so he sent a Redeemer. God sent his only Son, so that we might have life and have it more abundantly (John 10:10). That means that Christ, the Divine Physician, can heal not only our sinfulness but also our disordered passions, our irrational thoughts and moods, our past wounds, and our unhealthy, unbalanced emotional lives.

Christ wants us to be healed in this life. Christians do not have to wait until heaven to experience Christ's joy! As philosopher Peter Kreeft explains it,[101] from the perspective of eternity, everything *is!* So heaven can begin right now—albeit as a seedling or the mustard seed of which Jesus speaks. And just as a newly conceived baby in the womb is a human being *right now* and not a cat or a blob of tissue, so the joy of heaven can also begin *now*.

This does not mean that all of our problems will disappear, for Jesus warns us, "In the world you will have trouble" (John 16:33). And St. Paul writes: "We are afflicted in every way, but not constrained; perplexed, but not driven to despair; persecuted, but not abandoned; struck down, but not destroyed; always carrying about in the body the dying of Jesus, so that the life of Jesus may also be manifested in our body" (2 Corinthians 4:8-10). During his earthly ministry, Jesus healed many, yet he did not heal every suffering person (John 5:3-9). Christ has the power to heal us and transform us, but God's ways are mysterious. (As the poet William Cowper wrote, "God moves in a mysterious way / His wonders to perform.") God will always give us the grace we need to carry our crosses, but he may not heal us in the way we expect.

Perhaps we need to take a step in faith before experiencing the healing power of God. The woman with the hemorrhage touched the hem of Jesus' tunic, the man with the withered hand had to stretch out his hand, the paralyzed man had to pick up his mat. Sometimes our faith needs to grow before we can be healed. But always the healing of our souls is of primary importance. Faithful Catholics sometimes think they ought to be healed through the sacraments and prayer alone. But God's plan may indeed include wise earthly professionals, such as doctors, psychiatrists, and therapists. The paralyzed man was cured by Jesus after four friends broke through the roof and lowered him into the house (Mark 2:1-5). Scripture says, "Jesus saw *their* faith" (2:5, emphasis added).

You have probably heard the joke about the man who was hanging by his fingertips from a cliff, praying for God to save him. He turns down the offer of a rope, a helicopter, and a boat, crying out, "God will save me!" As he falls off the cliff, he asks why God had abandoned him. "I didn't abandon you," says God. "I sent you a rope, a helicopter, and a boat!"

DETACHING WITH LOVE*

Ultimately, only Christ can fill the void of existential isolation and free us from fear, anxiety, and resentment. "Christ strode

---

*We are indebted to Fr. Emmerich Vogt, OP, for his wisdom and teaching on detaching with love.

through the gate of our final loneliness. . . . In his Passion he went down into the abyss of our abandonment," writes Pope Benedict XVI.[102] Death no longer has power over us. But we have to let go of the habitual ways in which we try to assuage our loneliness, fear, shame, and emptiness. We need to empty ourselves of our attachments so that God can enter and fill us with his love. This is what detachment is all about. St. Teresa of Ávila says that detachment is one of the virtues we must practice in order to grow in the spiritual life and be able to pray properly. One way to encourage detachment is to remind ourselves that most of the things we are overly attached to will someday recede.[103] For example, while my reputation at work is important, it is not an absolute value; if I have put my work before God and my family, someday I will look back on it and realize that my family and God should have come first. This posture of looking at things from a more eternal perspective is not a flight into a spiritual wonderland but an honest assessment that many of the things I think I cannot live without are precisely things I can live without.

When Jesus tells us that to become his disciples, we must "hate" our father and mother, our brothers and sisters, our own children, and even our very selves (Luke 14:26), he does not mean that we should literally despise others. Nor does he want us to hate ourselves by crushing ourselves with low self-esteem or by becoming doormats to controlling people or victims to abusers of our goodwill. On the contrary, the gospel always emphasizes that we must love God, our neighbor, and ourselves.

Christians do not despise any good thing of this world (even money, food, or sex), but we should not be inordinately attached to them. Nor do we need to abandon our good and noble ideals—love, family, friendship, country, wisdom, and truth. God's love for us will never require us to abandon such good and noble ideals. What Jesus does mean is that we must always put God first and remain (lovingly) detached from everything that might possibly hinder our love for God. Detachment does not imply repression or amputation of our feelings; detachment with love means putting God first. We must love God above all things. "Love the Lord, your God, with all your heart, with all your being, with all your strength, and with all your mind" (Luke 10:27).

A rule of thumb with regard to any "worldly" good (whether wealth, status, or good health) is never to despise these good things but also never to actively desire them. Instead, we should be humbly grateful for both earthly and spiritual goods that God in his graciousness has bestowed upon us. There is a huge difference, Dietrich von Hildebrand points out, between having a "grateful joy" about our possessions and having a "desire for wealth."[104]

Jesus drives this point home in the parable of the rich man who has just had a bountiful harvest (Luke 12:16-21). Realizing his existing barns are too small, he decides to build larger barns in which to store the abundant grain (which sounds to us like a sensible decision), and then he says to himself, "You have so many good things stored up for many years, rest, eat, drink, be merry!" (12:19). We sympathize with the man; after all, he has just had a successful year, and he is wisely putting aside for the future and taking a much-needed break. He isn't defrauding his customers, "cooking" the books, or abusing his employees. Yet God says to him, "You fool, this night your life will be demanded of you" (12:20).

Rather than viewing this passage as a mandate against retirement plans, successful business ventures, or even vacation plans, we should understand it as a lesson about detaching with love. We must keep our success, wealth, or any good thing in its proper place—as a gift from God to be enjoyed but never at the expense of God himself. Jesus explains at the end of the parable: "Thus will it be for the one who stores up treasure for himself but is not rich in what matters to God" (Luke 12:21).

Detaching with love from our inordinate desires or passions, whether for material things or for status, prestige, control, or perfection, will ultimately free us to love more purely and joyfully. Detachment doesn't mean we can't love our children or our spouse or enjoy a beautiful sunset. In fact, love is the most fundamental of all emotions. According to Dietrich von Hildebrand, as we are gradually transformed in Christ, our hearts become even more sensitive, and we feel our emotions even more deeply. Yet these emotions and desires are purified of anything that is not good for us or others.[105] When we love God above all things, we incorporate our love for all good things here on earth into our love for God. When we lift our hearts in joy as we behold a spectacular sunset or a work of art, our minds can immediately be drawn to God in thanksgiving.

Detaching with love is a life's work. In addition to earthly attachments, there are the hidden attachments of our hearts, such as pride, self-love, vanity, and even our own will. When we are free from the tyrannical hold that our irrational thoughts, distraught emotions, evil habits, disordered attachments, overly sensitive feelings, past wounds, and fears have on us, we can more purely and joyfully love God and one another. Whether through the help of a professional therapist or through the aid of a trusted spiritual director (or both), we can begin to let go of the attachments and fears that hold us back. With abandonment to God's will and his love comes true and lasting peace.

HEALTHY AND HOLY LIVING

As we have noted in previous chapters, the emotions God gave us are vitally important. They are indicators that something important is happening that we need to attend to. They motivate us to take action, flee from danger, and desire the good. Our emotions are vital to our intimate relationships. Our Catholic faith does not ask that we repress our feelings or bottle them up or pretend that they don't exist. Through our emotions, we intuit the good and suspect evil. Our feelings are real; they are vital motivators, and they are a gift from God. But without the aid of our reason and God's grace, we cannot always rely on our emotions to guide us. Just because I feel strong emotions about something does not mean that I am necessarily right or correct. My strong feelings may or may not reflect reality. I need to listen to my feelings and make sense of them, and then take prudent action. Sometimes my out-of-control emotions may indicate an underlying trauma or emotional wound that needs to be addressed.

Sometimes our emotions make us want to respond with rage when someone cuts us off on the highway, scream at our children when they are not compliant, or give in to lust, gluttony, or envy. Our feelings can overtake our will if we let them. Instead, we are commanded to respond to the problems of life as Jesus did: with love (John 13:34; 15:12-13.) This is the great Christian gift to the world: to return any evil or misdeed with love. But in order to overcome my desire for revenge or payback, I have to die to myself, pick up my cross, and follow Christ. Instead of rolling my eyes and telling my spouse that I think he had a dumb idea, I should die to myself and listen with empathy instead of criticism. When I am cut off in traffic and barely avoid an accident, I resist the urge to hit the horn and curse, and I invite my family to say a prayer for this hurried and careless driver.[106] This is healthy Christian living.

As Christians, we have the wonderful gift of transforming our emotions through God's grace. We can experience a holy desire for God as well as delight in his word, deep sorrow for our sins, tender love and compassion for God's creatures, and sublime joy in God's presence. These and other emotions that are purely directed toward God inspire and motivate us to follow him ever more closely.

We hope that the preceding chapters have provided a practical way to understand your emotional life and to address some of the concrete situations that occur when your emotional life is out of control, unbalanced, or unhealthy. We have taken a look at how our temperaments, our irrational thoughts, our past emotional wounds, and our behavior can influence our emotional lives. Sometimes it will take the assistance of a professional to work through past trauma or present difficulties in order to regain perspective and a healthy emotional balance. Within the security of our families and with the help of our good friends and trusted professionals—and most important, with God's grace—we can begin to repair relationships that have been hurt through resentment or anger. We can begin to free ourselves from our deepest fears of abandonment, rejection, or worthlessness. We must let go of our unforgiveness, our resentment, our anger, and our past wounds and allow the mercy of God to flow. "Forgive us our trespasses, *as we forgive* those who trespass against us." Only when we show mercy will God be merciful to us. With God's mercy flowing through us, the healing will begin.

All this practical work needs to be done in the light of Christ. "In Christ human feelings are able to reach their consummation in charity and divine beatitude" (CCC, 1769). Christ's healing touch will allow us to truly experience the love of each Person of the Trinity—Father, Son, and Holy Spirit—as we are transformed from the clay of our weakened nature into the Trinitarian image once again: "Indeed, like clay in the hand of the potter, so are you in my hand" (Jeremiah 18:6).

GOING FURTHER

1. What attachments do you struggle with? Are you attached to material things, prestige, or power? Are you attached to being right, being in control, being liked, or being perfect? Or are you attached to overeating, drinking, or other vices? When circumstances threaten to take these away, do you become angry, fearful, or anxious? How can Christ help fill the void of emptiness, fear, and anxiety?

2. Jesus tells us to look at the birds in the sky and the lilies of the field (Matthew 6:25-34). God takes care of them, yet we are so much more important to God. He urges us to place our

trust in him and to depend on him completely. Our heavenly Father knows what we need. "But seek first the kingdom of God and his righteousness, and all these things will be given you besides" (Matthew 6:33). Placing our trust in God will help us let go of our unhealthy attachments. How can daily prayer and frequent reception of the sacraments help you in overcoming these attachments?

3. What steps can you take to become more emotionally balanced, forgiving, and free from past resentments? Before approaching the altar, Jesus reminds us that if you "recall that your brother has anything against you, leave your gift there at the altar, go first and be reconciled with your brother, and then come and offer your gift" (Matthew 5:23-24). Are there people in your life whom you need to forgive or ask forgiveness of? What other ways can you become more merciful, compassionate, and loving to those in your family and in your life? Bring your past resentments and hurts to Christ in prayer, and ask him for guidance, inspiration, and healing.

4. Depression, anger, resentment, and anxiety can imprison us spiritually and emotionally. We are less free to love God and our neighbor. We become isolated in our fear or anger. Do you feel imprisoned by these emotions? If so, seek the help of a wise priest and a Catholic therapist, and do not fear the light that Christ wants to shine in the darkness of despair or loneliness. Christ is calling us to transformation, to freedom, and to joy.

Endnotes

1. R. Joseph Massman wrote in 1941 in his classic *Nervousness, Temperament and the Soul* that "a human being almost always acts emotionally" (Fort Collins, CO: Roman Catholic Books, originally published in 1941), 15. His point is validated by contemporary author Jonah Lehrer, *How We Decide* (New York: Houghton Mifflin Harcourt, 2009), who points to neuroscientific research showing that every decision is accompanied by a wave of (sometimes unconscious) emotion.

2. It is not our intent to provide a comprehensive discussion of the exact nature of emotion; this is best left to philosophers and scientists. It suffices to say that philosophers and scientists agree that emotion involves a physiological process (the exact nature of which is in dispute). Most believe that a physiological process alone is not sufficient. Psychologist Jerome Kagan puts it this way: "A 'detected change in feeling' is a necessary but not sufficient feature of emotion. Thus, activation of the amygdala, in the absence of a felt change, would not *of itself* indicate the presence of an emotion." Jerome Kagan, *What Is Emotion?* (New Haven, CT: Yale University Press, 2007), 21–23.

3. Marcel Sarot, *God, Passibility and Corporeality* (The Netherlands: Pharos Publishing House, 1992), 116–117.

4. "May the God of peace himself make you perfectly holy and may you entirely, spirit, soul, and body, be preserved blameless for the coming of our Lord Jesus Christ."

5. Massman, *Nervousness, Temperament and the Soul*, 15.

6. Frank Sheed, *Theology and Sanity* (San Francisco: Ignatius Press, 1993), 184.

7. One wonders how Adam and Eve were tempted by Satan if they were such exceptional human beings. However, they were not "impeccable," which means they could commit sin. They were free to choose, and they chose evil.

8. Frank Moncher and Craig Steven Titus, "Foundations for a Psychotherapy of Virtue: An Integrated Catholic Perspective," *Journal of Psychology and Christianity*, Vol. 28, No. 1 (2009): 30.

9. The Douay-Rheims translation. Another translation says, "He ordered all my impulses." (Massman, *Nervousness, Temperament and the Soul*, 16).

10. Sometimes activating other emotions can transform the original (less desirable) emotions. For example, fear can be transformed by anger, and anger can be transformed by compassion. See Leslie Greenberg and Rhonda N. Goldman, *Emotion-Focused Couples Therapy* (Washington, DC: American Psychological Association, 2008), 22.

11. Chess and Thomas included approach/withdrawal categories in their temperament tests on babies, and Eysenck included the dimensions of introversion/extraversion in his Eysenck circle.

12. Paul Ekman, *Emotions Revealed*, 2nd ed. (New York: Henry Holt and Company, 2003), 64.

13. Paul McHugh, MD, and Philip Slavney, MD, *The Perspectives of Psychiatry*, 2nd ed. (Baltimore: John Hopkins Press, 1998), 132

14. In fact, this very point convinced renowned psychologist Jerome Kagan of Harvard University that temperament has an impact on a person's personality. Prior to this realization, he strictly ascribed to social determinism. As he reviewed a landmark study of infants who had been followed through adulthood, he realized that there was a group of shy, timid, somewhat anxious

adults who had been that way since they were born. This profoundly affected his thinking.

15. The landmark study by psychiatrists Stella Chess and Alexander Thomas, "The New York Longitudinal Study," identified nine temperamental categories in people from six months of age until their thirties. Stella Chess and Alexander Thomas, *Temperament in Clinical Practice* (New York: The Guilford Press, 1986).

16. Jerome Kagan, who has researched temperament for many years (though not the four classic temperament types that we are discussing here), points out that parenting styles can affect emotional development; for example, excessive criticism may cause a child to become more anxious. Other environmental factors such as trauma, war, or economic depression may also affect one's emotional development. Nonetheless, many temperamental biases persist throughout these environmental influences. Jerome Kagan, *The Long Shadow of Temperament* (Cambridge, MA: Harvard University Press, 2004), 24–26.

17. Kagan, *The Long Shadow of Temperament*, 226.

18. Kagan, *What Is Emotion?* 46.

19. "Nora" and all the following examples in this book are fictitious names, and the stories are composites of true cases in which details and specifics have been changed to protect confidentiality and to represent universal truths about our emotional lives.

20. Please be aware that depression is a mood disorder and requires professional attention. Nora is feeling particularly stressed and overwhelmed at this particular time, but if she begins experiencing clinical signs of depression that persist for several months, combined with other symptoms (such as overeating or loss of appetite, sleep problems, fatigue, poor self-esteem, or feeling hopeless), then she should seek professional help.

21. McHugh and Slavney, *The Perspectives of Psychiatry,* 141.

22. *The Temperament God Gave You* (2005) and *The Temperament God Gave Your Spouse* (2008) are published by Sophia Institute Press and can be found at www.sophiainstitute. com.

23. Henri Joly, *The Psychology of the Saints* (Fort Collins, CO: Roman Catholic Books, originally published in 1898), 47. The author points out that we might be inclined to doubt the saint's own words if this fact of his temperament were not confirmed by his close friends and companions.

24. Beverage alcohol causes everyone to be more extraverted, but in certain individuals who are already intense or unstable, this can cause rage and violence. McHugh, *The Perspectives of Psychiatry,* 135.

25. Leslie Greenberg, *Emotion-Focused Therapy* (Washington, DC: American Psychological Association, 2002), 5.

26. Dietrich Von Hildebrand, *The Heart: Source of Christian Affectivity* (Chicago: Franciscan Herald Press, 1977), 26.

27. Von Hildebrand, *The Heart: Source of Christian Affectivity,* 86–87.

28. Malcolm Gladwell, *Blink: The Power of Thinking Without Thinking* (New York: Little Brown & Co., 2005), 3ff.

29. Gladwell, *Blink: The Power of Thinking Without Thinking,* 59–60.

30. Daniel Goleman, *Social Intelligence* (New York: Bantam Books, 2006), 60–62.

31. Gladwell, *Blink: The Power of Thinking Without Thinking,* 44.

32. Greenberg, *Emotion-Focused Therapy,* 5.

33. Steven R. Covey, *The Seven Habits of Highly Effective People* (New York: Free Press, 1989, 2004), 30–31.

34. "We are all well aware that the roots of racism, xenophobia,

discrimination, and intolerance are found in ignorance, prejudice, and hatred, which may often arise from faulty and inadequate education." Michael Fitzgerald, "Intervention by the Holy See at the Organization for Security and Co-operation in Europe Conference on Tolerance and the Fight Against Racism, Xenophobia, and Discrimination," 2004, http://www.vatican.va/roman_curia/secretariat_state/2004/documents/rc_seg-st_20040914_osce-brussels_en.html.

35. Gladwell, *Blink: The Power of Thinking Without Thinking*, 241.

36. *Catechism of the Catholic Church*, 1787–1788, and Greenberg, *Emotion-Focused Therapy*, 6.

37. Greenberg, *Emotion-Focused Therapy*, 31. The study was Ekman and Friesen, 1975.

38. Ekman, *Emotions Revealed*, 78.

39. Ekman, *Emotions Revealed*, 69.

40. *The Summa Theologica of St. Thomas Aquinas*, 2nd and rev. ed., 1920, literally translated by the Fathers of the English Dominican Province, online ed. © 2008 by Kevin Knight, STI-II, q. 59, a. 2, http://www.newadvent.org/summa/2059.htm. St. Thomas is making the point that one can be virtuous and experience passion, but the passion should be "ordinate" or "as it should be in terms of manner and time."

41. Basil Maturin, *Self-Knowledge and Self-Discipline* (Harrison, NY: Roman Catholic Books, 1915), 51.

42. Fr. Emmerich Vogt, OP, "The Passions: A Guide for Understanding Your Feelings and Emotions," *The 12-Step Review*, 2000, http://www.12-step-review.org.

43. Von Hildebrand, *The Heart: Source of Christian Affectivity*, 57.

44. Reason alone may not be sufficient to transform unhealthy emotional responses into healthy ones, especially if there is a serious emotional wound. (See Greenberg and Goldman,

Emotion-Focused Couples Therapy.) We discuss emotional wounds in more detail in chapter 8.

45. "Blinded by Jealousy?" *Science Daily*, April 14, 2010, http://www.sciencedaily.com /releases/2010/04/100413160859.htm.

46. Claudia Wallis, "The New Science of Happiness," *Time* magazine, January 17, 2005.

47. *The Twelve-Step Review*, http://www.12-step-review.org.

48. Ratio of unpleasant to pleasant emotions is 2:1 (Greenberg, *Emotion-Focused Therapy*, 31).

49. Roy Baumeister et al., "Bad Is Stronger than Good," *Review of General Psychology*, Vol. 5, No. 4, 2001. In fact, the disproportionately strong reaction we have to something bad may have contributed to our evolutionary success, suggests Baumeister. If I fail to appreciate the good, I am merely missing out on something. If I fail to react appropriately to a threat, however, I may not survive. So survival favors the stronger effect of bad things.

50. Maturin, *Self-Knowledge and Self-Discipline*, 136ff.

51. Aaron Beck, *Depression: Causes and Treatment*, 2nd ed. (New York: The Guilford Press, 2009), xvii.

52. Patrick Carnes, *Out of the Shadows: Understanding Sexual Addiction*, 3rd ed. (Center City, MN: Hazelden Publishing, 2001), 152.

53. Maturin, *Self-Knowledge and Self-Discipline*, 151.

54. Maturin, *Self-Knowledge and Self-Discipline*, 152.

55. "Mood" here is understood as a continuous emotional state that does not have an object. For example, being in a "blue mood" is being continuously disposed to being sad, yet rarely can we identify a reason for or a target of our mood; this is in contrast to an emotion (for example, anger) that has a specific target or object (I am angry at my boss). Moods activate specific emotions. For example, if we are in a grumpy mood,

we are more likely to become angry when something annoys us. Perhaps this particular incident would not, if we were in a "good mood," have triggered our anger. (Ekman, *Emotions Revealed*, 50–51.)

56. Wallis, "The New Science of Happiness." We understand heredity to include temperament.

57. Wallis, "The New Science of Happiness."

58. Ekman, *Emotions Revealed*, 96.

59. Tara Parker-Pope, "Is Marriage Good for Your Health?" *New York Times Magazine*, April 12, 2010, http://www.nytimes.com/2010/04/18/magazine/18marriage-t.html.

60. Susan M. Johnson, *Emotionally Focused Couple Therapy with Trauma Survivors: Strengthening Attachment Bonds* (New York: The Guilford Press, 2002), 187.

61. John Paul II, *Original Unity of Man and Woman: Catechesis on the Book of Genesis*, (Boston: St. Paul Editions, 1981), 76.

62. Research on positive psychology and Dr. Martin Seligman's authentic happiness is presented in the *Time* magazine cover story, "The New Science of Happiness" by Claudia Wallis, January 17, 2005, http://www.authentichappiness.sas.upenn.edu/images/TimeMagazine/Time-Happiness.pdf.

63. Moncher and Titus, "Foundations for a Psychotherapy of Virtue: An Integrated Catholic Perspective," 22–35.

64. Martin Augustine Waldron, "Virtue," *The Catholic Encyclopedia*, Vol. 15 (New York: Robert Appleton Company, 1912), http://www.newadvent.org/cathen/15472a.htm.

65. *The Summa Theologica of St. Thomas Aquinas*, 2nd and rev. ed., STI-II, q. 59, a. 5.

66. Moncher and Titus, "Foundations for a Psychotherapy of Virtue: An Integrated Catholic Perspective," 22–35.

67. Meg Meeker convincingly presents much evidence for the

importance of dads in their daughters' lives. *Strong Fathers, Strong Daughters* (Washington, DC: Regnery Publishing, 2006).

68. Ekman, *Emotions Revealed*, 50–51. There are some moods that might require professional help: being in a depressed mood for a length of time or alternating euphoria with depression.

69. Ekman, *Emotions Revealed*, 23ff.

70. Romans 1:8ff; 1 Corinthians 1:4-6; Philippians 1:3-5; Colossians 1:3; 1 Thessalonians 1:2-4; 2 Thessalonians 1:3; Philemon 4; 2 Timothy 1:3, to cite a few examples.

71. Maturin, *Self-Knowledge and Self-Discipline*, 184.

72. Michael Potegal, Gerhard Stemmler, and Charles Spielberger, *International Handbook of Anger: Constituent and Concomitant Biological, Psychological, and Social Processes* (New York: Springer Publishing, 2010).

73. Jerome Kagan discusses some temperamental differences between Europeans and Asians in *The Long Shadow of Temperament*, 225ff.

74. Some studies show that venting may actually increase one's feeling of being angry rather than diffusing it. It is better to express anger appropriately: "That really upset me because . . . " to an empathetic listener. See John Gottman and Julie Schwartz Gottman, *Ten Lessons to Transform Your Marriage* (New York: Crown Publishers, 2006), 212.

75. Passive-aggressive behavior is often the result of not having learned how to "appropriately" deal with anger. We should learn (ideally as a youngster) how to express strong feelings appropriately (i.e., no name-calling, yelling, hitting, or taking it out on someone else). But if we were always taught that all strong feelings are bad, then we might not have learned how to do this appropriately. See Ross Campbell, *How to Really Love Your Teenager* (Wheaton, IL: Victor Books, 1981).

76. John Gottman and Julie Schwartz Gottman, *Ten Lessons to Transform Your Marriage*, 4ff.

77. Ekman, *Emotions Revealed*, 181.

78. Erasmo Leiva-Merikakis, *Fire of Mercy, Heart of the Word: Meditations on the Gospel According to Saint Matthew* (San Francisco: Ignatius Press, 1996), 220.

79. Vogt, "The Deadly Sin of Anger," *The Twelve-Step Review*, Winter 2010, http://www.12-step-review.org.

80. Maureen Canning, *Lust, Anger, Love: Understanding Sexual Addiction and the Road to Healthy Intimacy,* (Naperville: IL Sourcebooks, 2008), 100ff.

81. http://www.compassionpower.com.

82. Steven Stosny, *You Don't Have to Take It Anymore: Turn Your Resentful, Angry, or Emotionally Abusive Relationship into a Compassionate, Loving One* (New York: Free Press), 2006.

83. Stosny, *You Don't Have to Take It Anymore*, 16.

84. The four aspects of compassion do not need to be practiced in this order.

85. Brother Lawrence of the Resurrection, *The Practice of the Presence of God*, trans. Salvatore Sciurba, OCD (Washington DC: ICS Publications, 1994), 48.

86. This case (as are all the cases in this book) is a composite using a fictitious name and with the details altered to protect privacy and confidentiality.

87. John Eldredge's book *Fathered by God* (Nashville: Thomas Nelson, 2009) describes the important imprint of being beloved by one's father and the wounds that occur if this does not happen.

88. Meeker, *Strong Fathers, Strong Daughters*, 38.

89. Susan M. Johnson, *Emotionally Focused Couple Therapy with Trauma Survivors: Strengthening Attachment Bonds*, 182.

90. For the experience to be traumatic (whether a traumatic event or ongoing neglect), it usually involves both the feelings of helplessness and shame. The lack of support and feeling

responsible later affects the ability to regulate emotions, to have healthy intimacy, and to trust others.

91. Canning, *Lust, Anger, Love: Understanding Sexual Addiction and the Road to Healthy Intimacy*, 47.

92. Greenberg and Goldman, *Emotion-Focused Couples Therapy*, 60–61.

93. We are not advocating here an "attachment theory" of intimate relationships. Though childhood attachment bonds are important and may explain different styles of adult attachment as well as certain emotional styles (such as avoidant or anxious), love itself is likely far more complex than to be explainable solely in terms of an infant-caregiver relationship. (Greenberg and Goldman, *Emotion-Focused Couples Therapy*, 80–81).

94. For an indepth explanation of how spouses and family members can help create a supportive and secure environment, see Susan Johnson, *Emotionally Focused Couple Therapy with Trauma Survivors: Strengthening Attachment Bonds*, especially 115ff.

95. "Benedict XVI Points to Another Type of Healing," Zenit article, Sept. 15, 2008, http://www.zenit.org/article-23633?l=english.

96. Pope Benedict XVI comments at Lourdes in September 2008, Zenit article.

97. Anger and envy (certainly the sort that led to the murder of Abel) are, according to the Catechism, consequences of original sin (CCC, 2259).

98. Adolphe Tanquerey, *The Spiritual Life* (Rockford, IL: Tan Books [originally published in 1930], 2000), 789–793.

99. St. John of the Cross, *The Ascent of Carmel*, Bk I, C. VI.

100. Joseph Cardinal Ratzinger, *Introduction to Christianity* (San Francisco: Ignatius Press, 1990, 2004), 301.

101. Peter Kreeft, *Everything You Ever Wanted to Know about Heaven* (San Francisco: Ignatius Press, 1990), 175.

102. Ratzinger, *Introduction to Christianity*, 301.
103. Teresa of Ávila, *Way of Perfection*, trans. Fr. Kiernan Kavanaugh (Washington, DC: ICS Publications, 2000), 136.
104. Von Hildebrand, *The Heart: Source of Christian Affectivity*, 178.
105. Von Hildebrand, *The Heart: Source of Christian Affectivity*, 171.
106. This example, as well as much of this chapter, was inspired by the work of Fr. Emmerich Vogt, OP.

the WORD among us®
The Spirit of Catholic Living

This book was published by The Word Among Us. For nearly thirty years, The Word Among Us has been answering the call of the Second Vatican Council to help Catholic laypeople encounter Christ in the Scriptures—a call reiterated recently by Pope Benedict XVI and a Synod of Bishops.

The name of our company comes from the prologue to the Gospel of John and reflects the vision and purpose of all of our publications: to be an instrument of the Spirit, whose desire it is to manifest Jesus' presence in and to the children of God. In this way, we hope to contribute to the Church's ongoing mission of proclaiming the gospel to the world and growing ever more deeply in our love for the Lord.

Our monthly devotional magazine, *The Word Among Us*, features meditations on the daily and Sunday Mass readings, and currently reaches more than one million Catholics in North America each year and another 500,000 Catholics in 100 countries. Our press division has published nearly 180 books and Bible studies over the past 10 years.

To learn more about who we are and what we publish, log on to our Web site at **www.wau.org**. There you will find a variety of Catholic resources that will help you grow in your faith.

Embrace His Word, Listen to God . . .